THE
SILVER CHANTER

THE
Silver Chanter

HISTORICAL TALES *of*
SCOTTISH PIPERS

STUART McHARDY

BIRLINN

This edition first published in 2021 by
Birlinn Limited
West Newington House
10 Newington Road
Edinburgh
EH9 1QS

www.birlinn.co.uk

First published by Birlinn Ltd in 2004 as
The Silver Chanter and Other Piper Tales

ISBN 978 1 78027 722 6

British Library Cataloguing-in-Publication Data
A catalogue record for this book is available from the British Library

Typeset by Initial Typesetting, Edinburgh

FSC
www.fsc.org
MIX
Paper from
responsible sources
FSC® C018072

Printed and bound by Clays Ltd Elcograf S.p.A.

Contents

Introduction

⟫◆⟪

The sound of Scottish bagpipes skirling through the night to the accompaniment of the intricate and unique patterns of Scottish snare drumming is a sound that is known throughout the world. It is somewhat ironic that this widespread popularity of the Scottish bagpipes is a result of Scottish regiments going round the world as part of the expanding British empire. That same British state had destroyed the Highland society which many people today believe is the original home of the bagpipes. This is of course totally wrong. Bagpipes are no more Scottish in origin than they are Indian or Croatian.

Bagpipes are known in hundreds of different societies. The Czechs, French, Germans, Greeks, Hungarians, Italians and Spanish all have their own bagpipes and outside Europe they can be found in India and Tunisia. Bagpipes had also been popular in England up to the sixteenth century. There is a widespread misapprehension that the bagpipes are in some way 'Celtic' because people in areas where the Celtic languages were once, and in some cases still are spoken, all play the bagpipes. While this includes such putative Celtic areas as Galicia in the north-western corner of Spain, where they play the long-droned gaita, it takes no account of the fact that the Welsh, a vibrant Celtic-speaking culture, do not have the bagpipes. The confusion of ideas regarding notions of Celticity can best be summed up by the Interceltique Festival at L'Orient in Brittany. This marvellous annual event is a celebration of the cultures of the Celtic-speaking peoples, with a particular emphasis on bagpipes.

1

However, interviewing the pipe-bands representing Scotland in 1989 I discovered there was not one Gaelic-speaker among them – they were virtually all Scots speakers from Lowland areas, but dressed in the necessary kilts, bearskin hats etc. The dress of pipe bands is of course derived from the uniforms of the Highland Regiments of the British army and thus is hardly Scottish at all, even if the kilt was part of the traditional dress of the Scottish Highlander.

Despite the problems of Scottish history in general there is no doubt that the bagpipes are nowadays seen by many people throughout the world as being particularly Scottish. Pipers of course often play at weddings and I believe it says a lot for modern Scotland that a recent Sikh wedding in Edinburgh had the groom, in a golden turban, leaving the house for the marriage on a white horse – he and his brothers preceded by a piper and all of them in full Highland dress. The authenticity of modern Highland dress may be dubious but is now well-entrenched in Scottish society and it is a sign of a vibrant culture that it can change and develop rather than being rooted in an overly respectful attitude towards the past. But as ever in Scotland, there are always contradictions.

The point about the pipes not being a purely Highland instrument can be seen in 'Tam o'Shanter', one of the masterpieces of the incomparable poet Robert Burns.

There sat Auld Nick, in shape o beast,
A touzie tyke, black, grim and large,
To gie them music was his charge:
He screw'd the pipes an gart them skirl,
Till roof and rafters aw did dirl.

Here he is satirising the Scottish idea of the devil, someone far removed from His Satanic Majesty, the personification of all evil, and the familiar term 'Auld Nick' shows a being that can be treated humorously. The point here is that Auld Nick is playing at Auld Alloway Kirk, in Ayrshire on Scotland's southwest coast, far from the Scottish Highlands.

Pipers were never limited to the Highland areas of Scotland. In the Lowlands in the sixteenth century and later, many towns had an official piper whose role was to play through the streets every morning and evening at specified times as a means of public time-keeping. Effectively they woke the people up and later told them what time to go to bed. They would also play at regular events like feasts and fairs. While many of these town pipers did not survive beyond the seventeenth century, in some places the pipers held their positions; the Jedburgh pipers – the Hastie family – stayed on till 1790, and some pipers survived even longer. The position of town piper often included both a wage and a house. We have no records or traditions in the Lowlands of the schools of piping like that attributed to the MacCrimmons, or of any particular master pipers. The musicians would of course have had to have been instructed by someone, but we do not hear of any outstanding individual pipers in the Lowland areas. Their job was essentially to provide music for the community, something that can be said of pipers within Highland society too, even if the social occasions which called for pipers might vary. Much has been made of the piper's role in Highland society since the early nineteenth century, but like much else from that period pertaining to Highland society, there has been a great deal of romanticising. There are stories here of Lowland origin and it is clear from what records we have that piping was widespread and common throughout Scotland from the Middle Ages onwards.

The History of the Bagpipe

Bagpipes are known in much of the world. Trying to figure out where and when they were first invented is an exercise in futility.

Representations of bagpipes have been found in the Middle East and Egypt from the second millennium BC and there are mentions of the instrument in the Bible. Some records tell of the Chinese having a bagpipe as early as 2585 BC; it was known in ancient India and there are also classical Greek references to bagpipes. It is therefore quite obvious that bagpipes have developed in many different parts of the world over a long time and to try and find out how they came to Scotland, far less where they were first played, is a hopeless task. Due to the way western culture has developed there has long been a particular fascination with the civilisations of Greece and Rome. This has led to the suggestion that the Romans must have brought the bagpipes to Scotland because we have representations of bagpipes in a Roman carving at Richmond Castle in Kent and another from Stanwix, near Carlisle, a fort on Hadrian's Wall. Another similar carving was found near Bo'ness on the river Forth in 1870 and there have been suggestions that the bagpipe was the favoured instrument of the Roman infantry just as the cavalry used the trumpet. The existence of the bagpipes before the first century is mentioned by the Greek playwright Aristophanes in his work *The Acharnians*, where he wrote, 'You pipers who are here from Thebes, with bone pipes blow the posterior of a dog.' This could be a reference to a skin bag. There was one very famous piper in Rome – Nero, who considered himself a good piper. During his reign the bagpipes were even included on a coin. Dio Chrysostom wrote in AD 115, 'They say he can . . . play the aulos both with his mouth and also with his armpit, a big bag being thrown under it.'

The lack of early written references to the bagpipe in Scotland has led to suggestions of it being imported at a later date but we should remember that, due to ongoing struggles with her southern neighbour, Scotland has very few early written sources. The invasions of both Edward I and Oliver Cromwell, nearly four hundred years apart, both saw widespread destruction of indigenous written material. When you add in the destruction that accompanied the Reformation in Scotland, when many churches, the natural places for old records to survive, were vandalised, it is easy to understand the lack of early Scottish documentation.

For a long time in the western world it has been the norm to see 'civilisation' and 'progress' as something that spread out from the Mediterranean cultures to the barbarians in the north and west. While writing and the development of cities were undoubtedly spread with the advance of the Roman empire, the idea that we in Scotland were unenlightened savages awaiting education at the hands of the invading Romans is an insult. We also have a problem in understanding the past in that it became the norm in European universities to stress the influence of classical culture. The notion that there is no significant culture without writing has led to suggestions that Scotland was an isolated and backward wee country far behind the Mediterranean centres of civilisation. This is demonstrably untrue as there were great megalithic structures like Calanais in Lewis and Maes Howe in Orkney being raised in the fourth millennium BC, before the Egyptians started building their pyramids. Recent research underlines the reality that sea transport was extensive in such distant times and that cultural exchange was the norm over wide areas. Widespread evidence suggests that there was some form of bagpipe in use over much of Europe when the Romans began to create their empire. If one person has an idea in one place it is quite likely that someone else will have the same idea somewhere else, and the wide variety of types of bagpipe would suggest that far from being local responses to outside influences, they are in fact local variants on a common approach to musical development.

Given that in Scotland a carnyx, a sophisticated bronze Caledonian war trumpet dating back to the first century AD, was found on the shores of the Moray Firth, it seems just as likely that there would have been an indigenous form of the bagpipe at that time in Scotland. There is also a carved stone representation of a man playing a double pipe on a Pictish symbol stone from St Vigeans at Arbroath. This seems likely to have been a pipe with a drone, suggesting that early in the first millennium AD some of the technology of the bagpipe was in use in Scotland.

The earliest specific evidence for the bagpipe in Scotland is thought to be two sculptures that used to be visible at Melrose Abbey. This is mentioned by Dalyell in his *Musical Memoirs* of 1849. One of these carvings was of a pig playing the pipes and Manson in *The Highland Bagpipe* mentioned a tradition that it was carved during the reign of James IV as a satire on the Highlanders. While there is no doubt that the Stewart monarchs were in a constant struggle with the Highland clans, the idea of the pipes being specifically associated with the Highlands in this period cannot be sustained.

The bagpipe was still used in England in the time of Chaucer and the tradition of the Lowland pipes is itself of considerable antiquity. Again in this respect we should remember that bellows pipes are a variation of the same basic idea of the bagpipe. The Lowland, Border and Northumbrian piping traditions are as authentic as those of the Highlands and the notion that they are separate and distinct traditions arises from an obsession with differentiating people on the grounds of language. While much of the tradition of the Highland pipes developed among Gaelic speakers and that of the Borders amongst Scots speakers, the idea that people speaking different languages are separated in a similar fashion to people living along the borders of modern nation states is somewhat simplistic. The norm for many human beings in much of the world is not to speak just one language but rather to speak two or more. Professor Sandy Fenton made a telling point at the conference founding the Elphinstone Institute in the 1990s when he said to forget the Highland line, and to think of a Highland sausage – an area where two overlapping language groups share various aspects of culture and social existence.

The world-famous fifteenth-century Rosslyn Chapel near Edinburgh has carvings of pipers and piping, and we have growing references to the use of pipes amongst the Highland clans from the fourteenth century onwards. Traditions that survived amongst the Macdonald and Menzies clans maintained that their ancestors were playing the pipes at Bannockburn.

The Scottish bagpipe is undoubtedly the best-known form of bagpipe in the world. While all bagpipes are a development of earlier blown pipes – the bag allowing both continuous playing and considerably more volume than the lungs themselves – the Scottish bagpipe has become known all over the world because of its use by the British army. In country after country the Scottish regiments were the shock troops of the British empire and the massed pipes of the army bands have had an incredible effect on peoples of all religions, races and cultures. This is somewhat ironic when one considers that the people amongst whom the 'piob mhor' developed – the tribal peoples of the Scottish Highlands – were discouraged by the government from playing it themselves in the aftermath of the Jacobite rebellion of 1745–53. The Disarming Acts of 1746 banned the carrying of arms and the wearing of the kilt, while the playing of bagpipes, like other aspects of ancient Highland culture, was actively discouraged, though not specifically banned. Many commentators mention the fact that as a musical instrument of war, the 'great pipes' of the Highlands were without equal. The loud and shrill notes of the bagpipe, sometimes likened by those unappreciative of their majesty to the caterwauling of cats, could be heard above the noise of hand-to-hand fighting and can carry up to ten miles in favourable climatic conditions.

The banning of traditional Highland weapons and dress in the Disarming Act can, in today's terms, be seen as a deliberate attempt at cultural annihilation, even if it did not specify the bagpipes as an instrument of war. From the 1730s onwards, when General Wade began driving modern metalled roads into the

Scottish Highlands, the days of Highland society, the last Celtic-speaking warrior society of Europe, were numbered. British society was shaken to the core in 1745 by how close the Highland army, with its pipers, came to taking over London and reimposing the Stewart monarchy. However in the aftermath of this struggle, which carried on in a desultory guerrilla campaign in the Highlands till the mid-1750s, the British army continued to use the bagpipes in the regiments that had been raised from the Highland regions. The tradition of the pipes stirring up the Highland warriors to battle was adapted by the expanding military machine of the British empire, with great effect.

It is one of the ironies of history that in the modern world the pipes have become synonymous with Scottish Highland culture throughout the world. Despite their assault on Highland Gaelic society the British government fully appreciated the power of the pipes in battle and the Scottish Highland regiments, raised from the 1730s onwards, were allowed to use them throughout the period. They were also allowed to wear a form of their traditional dress, though it was banned in the Highlands. This is not quite as anomalous as it seems. We should remember that the Jacobite rebellions of the eighteenth century were in reality part of an ongoing civil war and that some of the worst atrocities committed in the Highlands after Culloden were perpetrated by Scotsmen. There were Highlanders and Lowlanders, and pipers, on both sides.

The army pipers must have helped to preserve the role of piping within Scottish society as a whole, for Highland pipers in the British army often returned home to Scotland; it is stretching belief to think not one of them would have played a note out of uniform over the period. During the period 1746–53, when the British army garrisoned virtually the entire Highlands of Scotland and her major cities, there was probably a substantial falling-off in bagpipe-playing by 'civilians' but, just as weapons were hidden, so bagpipes must have been, and once the troops left the glens it seems likely that pipers would have gone back to their playing. It is not difficult to envisage a scene where the British army garrison departed from a glen in the early 1750s and immediately a set of pipes appeared and music was played in celebration.

One view of history tries to suggest that the '45 was a struggle between Scotland and England. It was not. Scots and English fought on both sides and were driven by religious and political beliefs. The end result, however, was that the Highlands – where for centuries both Edinburgh and London had been unable to impose their will – were changed for ever and a society that in many ways preserved ancient continuities with the Iron Age disappeared.

With the revival of interest in all things 'Celtic', a word that would have meant nothing to any of the Celtic-speaking peoples before 1700, piping became very popular in the early nineteenth century. This was partly due to the romanticised vision of Highland society presented by Sir Walter Scott. His organisation of the royal visit of 1822, when George IV went out and about in Edinburgh in a kilt (and pink tights!), helped to make such interest fashionable. It would, however, be wrong to dismiss the vigour of indigenous culture in the second half of the eighteenth century as being solely inspired by such romanticism. A strange form of nationalism had developed in which the poet Robert Burns, a radical freethinker and avid supporter of the French Revolution, could pen songs in support of the Jacobite cause. The Jacobites had supported the Stewarts, a dynasty well known for their scorn of Gaelic culture, belief in the divine right of kings and latterly, total indifference to Scotland. This strange combination of beliefs stemmed from a variety of causes: the resentment of the corruption that led to the Union of the Parliaments in 1707; the lack of benefits for most of the population from that union; the revulsion at the activities of the British army after

Culloden; and probably partially from nostalgia as shown in the very idea of Auld Lang Syne – a vague time in the past when life was much better than the present.

By the mid-nineteenth century Romanticism had taken over and what is know seen as tartan kitsch was in full swing. The creation of the modern formal Highland dress, while based on the philabeg or little kilt – the full plaid was the philamore, or great kilt – is a nineteenth-century invention. Piping, with the pipers wearing the militarised derivative of actual Highland dress devised by the British army, became a very obvious symbol of this touristic version of Scottish culture. However, in amongst all this, the revival of piping, despite the myths and fantasies, did represent a new flowering of Scottish music. It has long been accepted wisdom amongst writers on piping that the tradition survived through the Middle Ages due to the patronage of Highland chiefs. I would suggest that this is only part, and probably a small part, of the story.

The Construction of the Bagpipe

The basic construction of the bagpipe consists of

- a chanter
- a bag of skin or leather
- a mouthpiece
- a set of drones, nowadays three but originally just one

The chanter is the part of the instrument played by the fingers and contains a double reed. It has seven finger-holes and a thumb-hole, and has a usual range of an octave and one note. It is attached to a skin bag, which allows a continuous supply of air to be maintained by the player through the mouthpiece. This contains a round piece of leather hinged onto the bag end which acts as a one-way valve. As the player blows air in, the flap opens;

when he stops blowing the air pressure within the bag forces the flap shut – as opposed to playing a fife or whistle directly with air from the lungs. Early pipes, which survive in different parts of Europe like the Balkans and Galicia, have a single drone, a device which lets the player finger the tune to an accompanying steady note. This is the earliest form of the bagpipe and was in use in Scotland as late as the sixteenth century. By squeezing the bag with his left hand while a breath is taken, the piper can keep up a flow of air in both the drone pipe(s) and chanter. The drones, two tenor and one bass, each have their own double reed. It seems likely that the first pipes in Scotland, no matter how they got here, would have been single drone pipes. The development of a two-drone pipe in Scotland happened in the first half of the sixteenth century. Adding a second tenor drone gave the pipes a richer harmonic complexity. The addition of a third drone, a bass drone, making the great pipes as we know them today, didn't take place till the early 1700s. This further increased the harmonic depth of the instrument and of course also greatly increased the volume of the pipes. Previous to this there was a mention of the 'great pipes' in 1623 but this probably referred to a two-drone set. Given the problems later associated with the pipes, it is noteworthy that in 1623 the piper playing the great pipes at Perth was prosecuted for playing his instrument on a Sunday and thus profaning the Sabbath.

The Music of the Pipes

PIBROCH

The Gaelic word 'piobaireachd', now 'pibroch' in Scots and English, means 'what a piper does' and underlines the importance of the classical pibroch tradition in the history and development of the Highland bagpipe over the past couple of centuries. Today a pibroch consists of an 'urlar', Gaelic for ground, which presents the theme, followed by a series of variations of increasing complexity on that theme. Once the piper has exhausted the tune, or his own possibilities for variation, he returns to the theme before finishing the piece. Around three hundred old pibrochs have been preserved. Among the oldest are thought to be 'The Battle of Harlaw' (1411), 'Black Donald's March to the Isles' (1427), 'The End of the Great Bridge' (1427), 'MacRae's March' (1491), 'The Park Piobaireachd' (1491), 'MacIntosh's Lament' (1526), 'The Battle of Waternish' (1578), and 'Hector MacLean's Warning' (1579). The dates are in fact speculative. Some pibrochs have also been used as tunes within the song traditions of both Gaelic and Scots. In the aftermath of the 1746 Disarming Acts a whole generation was discouraged from playing the pipes outside the army and it seems certain that in this period many great tunes were lost forever. The piping tradition in Scotland, having survived the Disarming Acts, has developed with levels of commitment and seriousness that have led to the claim that the old pibrochs have survived as they used to be played, note for note, thus preserving the ancient authenticity of the tradition even as it continued to develop. This idea is hard to sustain, given the effectiveness of the Disarming Acts, and people may believe it or not as they will. In recent years the innovations of player/composer Martyn Bennett serve to show that this ancient tradition still has plenty of potential for future development, even for young audiences raised on a diet of electronic music.

Pibroch can be understood as the classical music of the Highland bagpipe although the instrument can of course be used in many other settings. Weddings, funerals, dances and parades have all been using pipers, either solo or in bands with drummers, for a long time in Scotland. The repertoire of Scottish music suitable for the pipes consists of reels, Strathspeys, schottisches and marches, many of which are extremely popular. All Scottish piping music arises from our traditional indigenous music and, while no one can dispute the majesty and wonder of good pibroch playing, to suggest that its origin is different from 'ceol beg', the little music, comprising dances, marches, airs etc, is unsustainable. We have no definitive proof of the origin of 'ceol mor', the big music. Opinion amongst many music historians is that the development of ceol mor, with pibroch at its heart, came about after the final development of what we today think of as the classic Scottish Highland bagpipe with its three drones. This only happened in the seventeenth century. In a contradiction that is typically Scottish, while pibroch is uniquely Scottish and has its roots in traditional Scottish music, its great flowering since the early years of the nineteenth century owes a great deal to the Highland Societies which were formed from amongst the middle classes of Scotland and England and were driven by an overly-romanticised idea of Scottish history.

Ceol Beg

Literally meaning 'the little music', this is the term used to describe the music most people associate with the pipes – reels, strathspeys, marches and jigs, as well as song tunes. The reels, strathspeys and jigs are dance music, Scotland having long had a vibrant dance tradition. Reels were the most common form of dance and it is likely that the name was originally Norse. The great flowering of culture under the Lordship of the Isles in the late Middle Ages drew on both Norse and Gaelic traditions, language and culture. Dancing seems to have always been popular in the Highlands and it was considered a manly art amongst the warriors of the clan. Nowadays it is believed that the Highlanders used a set of pipes smaller than the full Highland bagpipe for accompanying dancing. It is also worth noting that for much of the year Highland weather can be somewhat unpleasant and playing the full Highland bagpipes in a 'tigh dubh' (traditional Highland black house) with its low roof would have been a painful experience for all present. The smaller pipes could be used indoors and there have been suggestions that some of the smaller pipes might have been bellows-driven, as in the Borders and Northumbria. Today the bagpipes are used to accompany competition dancing, particularly in the dozens of Highland Games that still take place all across Scotland every summer.

These games also have piping competitions, which are taken very seriously by all involved, no matter how small a gathering they take place at. These piping and dancing competitions show the dynamism and health of traditional Scottish culture. Though many of the bigger gatherings attract hosts of tourists, most of the smaller events are run solely for the benefit of the local population, and competitors in the various competitions often come a good distance to compete. Collections of ceol beg were relatively rare until the later years of the nineteenth century, after which many collections were published based on the repertoires of the pipe bands of the various Scottish regiments. Here again the influence of the British army pipe bands was of considerable importance. While pibroch can be seen as the classical music of the pipes, ceol beg fulfils the role of popular music, if such differentiations have any real meaning. Most pipe bands and individual pipers play ceol beg but the pibroch tradition of ceol mor continues to have a central role in modern piping. Much of the ceol beg tradition, like all traditional or folk music, has come down to us from an indeterminate time in the past, and though many of the tunes are now available as written music, their survival formerly depended on being passed from piper to piper.

CANNTAIREACHD

Already in the sixteenth century pipe masters and their pupils were using a sing-song that could imitate and convey both the pitch and length of the notes as well as all the grace notes that would occur in the pieces to be played on the Scottish bagpipes. Work on transcribing the pieces preserved orally in canntaireachd did not start until the nineteenth century. It appears to have begun with the publication of a small book written in 1828 by

Neil MacLeod of Gesto, known generally, in the Scottish fashion, by the place he inhabited, as Gesto. He was a bit of an eccentric with a taste for litigation, particularly against MacLeod of MacLeod. However, the transcription of what was probably an individual style of using vocables to represent the tunes has since become rigid. We should remember that the canntaireachd arose from within a society in which oral transmission was the norm. The idea that there could be a single codified system of representing the wide variety of tunes played on the bagpipes is difficult to prove. Piping is a form of music that despite its codification and structuring since the early 1800s arose within the wider folk music tradition of Scotland and would therefore have strong regional stylistic variations.

The Clans

Many writers on the bagpipes in Scotland have emphasised the role of the piper as a servant of the chief. Particularly in the nineteenth century the belief arose that the Highland clan system was inherently feudal. The idea of the clan chief as some sort of feudal overlord of all the clan is not borne out by what we actually know about clan society. The chief's role, like that of the piper, was bound by unwritten rules developing from the social organisation of the clan itself, a kin-group arrangement that was in some ways more like that of the North American plains tribes than any form of feudalism. One well-known incident shows that the chiefs were far from hereditary despots. A young chief of the MacDonalds was brought back on the death of his predecessor from the clan with whom he had been fostered. When he saw the great feast arranged to honour him he made the unfortunate comment that a few hens would have done as well as the deer, oxen, sheep and other game that had been cooked. He was immediately taken off the clan lands and his brother substituted as clan chief. He did not understand that the investiture of a new chief was of central importance to the entire clan and that as chief he was answerable to the clan, as they were to him. The fact that most clan chiefs were known simply as, for example, 'The MacDonald' or 'The Chisholm' is a clear manifestation of tribal reality within the clan system. The chief was the closest direct descendant of the original clan founder and as such was both leader and representative of the entire kin-group that formed the clan. People coming into specific clan areas could take on the name of the local clan and be treated as full members. Rennie, in *The Scottish Nation* mentions that on several occasions chiefs who misruled were 'removed'. Partly due to the highly roman-ticised writings of Sir Walter Scott and partly to the fashion for all things Highland that he stimulated after the royal visit of George IV in 1822, the idea that the chiefs treated their clans-people as little more than serfs became widespread.

The reality was different, as is shown by the following from Burt's *Letters from a Gentleman,* a collection of letters from the 1730s. He tells us about the Highlanders' relationship with their chief :

> ... and as the meanest among them pretend to be his Relations by Consanguinity, they insist upon the Privilege of taking him by the Hand whenever they meet him. Concerning this last, I once saw a Number of very dis-contented Countenances when a certain Lord, one of the Chiefs, endeavoured to evade this Ceremony. It was in Presence of an English Gentleman in high station, from whom he would have willingly have concealed the Knowledge of such seeming Familiarity with slaves of so wretched Appearance, and thinking it, I suppose, as a kind of Contradiction to what he had often boasted at other Times, viz., his despotic Power over his Clan.

It is noticeable that he says that it is the member of the clan who was insisting on his right to shake his chief's hand. While this does not mean that the two were absolute equals it does show that within the tribal/clan system there was a social system totally unlike that of England where there were aristocracy, gentry and, effectively, serfs, or as Burt himself put it, slaves. There is a level of egalitarianism that not only contradicts but has no obvious precursors in feudalism. The supposed absolute power of the Scottish chief over his clansmen does not fit in with this eyewitness account. The piper's role in earlier times was probably more akin to that of the town piper in the Lowland areas in that he had a role within the clan system as a whole, both for entertainment at a range of social occasions, providing the music at important events and marching into battle. The idea that the Highland pipers were the personal servants of the chiefs comes from the period after the clan system had gone into decline and the chiefs were more concerned with their rents than their relations – who at one point were the entire clan. The chief was the centre of much of the social, economic and even ritual activity of the clan and the piper's role would be closely involved with such activities.

Language

Many of the tales here were originally in Gaelic and have become part of the wider Scottish tradition through translation into Scots or English. Others, from the Lowland areas, would have originated in Scots. Both Gaelic and Scots have been spoken in Scotland for more than 1,500 years, while English as it is spoken today in Scotland has come in over the past three or four centuries. Stories survive in the everyday languages that people speak and no one language is a guarantee of a story's authenticity. Some people like to think that Scots is a direct descendant of English and thus is a less truly indigenous language than Gaelic. In fact Scots comes from the same roots as English but developed separately from it. Both Scots and English are Germanic languages and we know that Germanic tribes were fighting in Scotland alongside both P-Celtic (Welsh) and Q-Celtic (Gaelic) speaking tribes, as far back as the fourth century, so to claim one language as being of more antiquity or authenticity than another is to misunderstand history.

Story

The material in this book comes from traditional tales that have in the main been written down over the past century or so. It is only recently that the role of storytelling has begun to be understood. While there has always been an awareness that the oral tradition contained remnants of ancient beliefs, it is now understood that in some cases story can pass on hard facts over periods that can be as long as thousands of years. While historians tend to concentrate on the written word to tell us of our past and archaeologists rely on physical artefacts, stories have probably been told for as long as human beings have had the power of language. The process of storytelling was how knowledge was passed on from generation to generation, whether it was practical knowledge, mythology and ritual, or tales of heroes and heroines. Such tales continue to be told for as long the audience finds them relevant and are not necessarily superseded by the arrival of literacy. There is at the moment a worldwide resurgence of interest in storytelling and we are only now beginning to understand that these remnants of the past can teach us a great deal about our ancestors. We should remember that even today in the modern western world not everyone can read and write. Just a couple of hundred years ago literacy was often very limited amongst the rural and urban working classes. So although the storytelling tradition was not as structured as it had been in earlier times it continued to flourish.

Even today you hear people in pubs, at parties and other social gatherings who are natural storytellers and often the stories they tell are based on traditional material – old tales in new clothes. The historians' obsession with paper and dates has blinded us to the fact that oral transmission retains a great deal of what life was like for our ancestors and how they themselves saw the world they inhabited. One type of common piping tale illustrates this very well (see 'A Long Night's Playing'). This story type also includes fiddlers and other musicians in different local traditions. Basically, the story is that a couple of pipers are on their way home from a wedding or other social event, when they come upon a fairy hill with its door wide open. The fairies invite them in and get them to play throughout the night, plying them with high-quality whisky, and in the morning they are sent on their way. They find themselves in a world totally unlike the one they had left and in some cases they are said to have been in the fairy hill for a century or more. Once they realise what has happened they usually crumble away to dust. Variants of this story continued to be told well into the twentieth century, with the version told here having the pipers coming across motorcars in the streets of Inverness when all they had known was horse transport.

It seems at least possible that the 'pipers in the fairy mound' stories contain echoes of ancient rituals at burial chambers – fairy mounds in local stories often turn out to be burial mounds. Similarly there are legends of hollow hills where Arthur or Finn MacCoul lie sleeping, accompanied by armed warriors awaiting a summons to come forth to save the land. Such hills are often associated with the old pagan communal fire festivals of Beltane (1st May) and Samhain (Soween), or Hallowe'en. If there is anything to this suggestion, the type of instrument played by the musicians in such tales has probably changed over the hundreds and hundreds of years these stories have been told. However, it does underline that the bagpipes are an integral part of Scottish culture and have been so for some considerable time.

Different versions of the same basic tales crop up in a variety of places. This is because for maximum impact stories were set within the known environment of the audience. This would be particularly important for children, who would be given most of their moral and social education through the medium of story-telling. For maximum effect it was best if the stories and their characters inhabited the landscape that the children knew. It is because of this need that there are so many different locales where, for example, stories of King Arthur survive in Britain, several of them in Scotland. People in many parts of Scotland, Wales and Cornwall spoke similar Brythonnic languages up to about a thousand years ago, languages which were the ante-cedents of modern Welsh. This is something that is only now beginning to be truly understood – in the past the similarity be-tween stories told in Scotland to others from England, Germany or Greece was explained as having come about by someone bringing the story here. The existence of many instances of Finn MacCoul stories surviving in the Gaelic-speaking population of the west has been said to be a result of the Gaels having come initially from Ireland. Recent research shows categorically that the ancient Gaelic-speaking kingdom of Dalriada was not founded by settlers from Ireland. People speaking the same language tend to have the same legendary and mythological stories and cultural contact is a complex process. The cultural situation vis à vis Scotland and Ireland is better regarded as being a two-way street.

Stories can, however, also have something to teach the modern world. In this respect it is worth remembering that the discovery of the ancient Greek city of Troy came about through the German amateur archaeologist Schliemann following up the literary references in Homer's *Iliad* – references which historians and archaeologists of the time had no doubt were derived from earlier oral tradition and thus fictional. Written literature has only been around for a few thousand years, one of the earliest examples of writing coming from ancient Mesopotamia, modern Iraq, from about 3500 BC, but humans have been on the planet since long before then. It is plain that for most of that time people have been handing down stories from one generation to the next.

Stories survive in different locales, and in various languages and cultures, because they address common human understanding. There are some stories from Australia's aboriginal Dreamtime that tell of giant marsupial creatures. Dismissed as fantasy for many years, the bones of these creatures began to turn up during mining operations in the 1950s. When they were dated they turned out to be over 30,000 years old and many were found near what were clearly hearth fires. Stories about them had survived by oral transmission for all that time. While our piping tales are of course much more recent than that, some of them are certainly part of a continuum of tradition that is truly ancient. In how they tell us of the people involved and the society they inhabited they retain the capacity to speak to those of us ready to listen.

In the latter half of the twentieth century storytelling became the focus of considerable academic research in Scotland and the extent of the treasure that was held by various communities began to be realised. One of these communities was Scotland's travelling people, many of whom have for centuries wandered all over both Scotland and Ireland. Some of the stories retold here are from that tradition, while others come from mainly rural locations amongst both Gaelic and Scots speakers. Yet others have been gleaned from local histories and literary collections. Stories from the distant past have survived alongside stories from more modern times, and both types appear here. As interest in storytelling grows we are beginning to appreciate what these tales can tell us of our history, and what life was like for our ancestors. History itself has until recently been concerned with the activities of the 'high heid yins', kings and nobles, soldiers, religious leaders and the rich. As social history becomes more developed the storytelling tradition can help to remind us that the material used by historians refers to no more than a tiny portion of human society at any one time. Tales can be seen as telling us the true story of the common people, to a certain extent in their own words. Stories survive because people still want to hear them. And in Scotland the pipes have always been important to the people playing them and the people listening to them, not just to the lairds who could afford to maintain a professional piper. In his book *The MacCrimmon Legend*, Campsie inadvertently shows the limitations of what one might call the 'educated' attitude towards Highland society. He tells us:

> The nation was wholly illiterate. Neither bards nor seannachies could write or read; but if they were ignorant, there was no danger of detection; they were believed by those whose vanity they flattered.

This statement misses the point spectacularly. He refers to the seannachies in a note as 'storytellers', but they were in fact also the guardians of the genealogies of the clans, a matter of great importance in a tribal society claiming descent from an original common ancestor. We should remember that it was this shared common ancestry amongst all the people of a clan that made the role of the bards and the seannachies central to clan society. Campsie, in assuming that there was something feudal about clan structure, misses the fact that in general the seannachies would not be able to simply flatter the chiefs – their responsibility was to the entire clan and in many cases they were raised to fulfil a hereditary role, being trained in the necessary memory skills from a very early age. In this respect they were perhaps more like the ancient druids than the flattering sycophants of a medieval feudal court.

The repetition of a traditional story in oral-based societies is something different from mere entertainment, in that its authenticity is a matter of importance for the entire group. There would always be people present who themselves had considerable knowledge of traditional story, as well as the bard or seannachie. In fact because of the nature of oral tradition the same stories would have been told and retold and most, if not all, of the social group would have a considerable knowledge of them, making it virtually impossible to alter or distort the inherent matter of such stories.

The Stories

Some of the stories in this book provide examples of motifs which occur in different parts of Scotland. I have reworked them without, I hope, taking away any of their essence. The tale 'A Long Night's Playing' is known in several versions – some of them make the musicians fiddlers rather than pipers – while 'The Piper of Keils' employs a motif that turns up in other places in Scotland where there are caves – on Tiree and at Dickmontlaw in Angus, for example. As already suggested, the possibility exists that stories of the musicians in the fairy hills and perhaps even the pipers in caves might hark back to ancient practices. The entertainment aspect of traditional storytelling has been exaggerated; the stories were always much more than mere entertainment. But I hope that the tales in this collection will entertain you, and hopefully, now and again, perhaps inform you as well.

The MacCrimmons

<hr/>

The MacCrimmons are the most famous of all the Scottish pipers. The stories here are only some of the traditional material regarding these hereditary pipers of the MacLeod clan on Skye. There has been much argument over the years as to the authenticity of the MacCrimmon story and Alistair Campsie suggested in his book on them that not only was their role heavily exaggerated, but that the famous piping school at Boreraig was a fiction. While the MacCrimmons have probably been romanticised as a result of the Victorian upsurge of interest in all things Highland, there can be little doubt that they lived at Boreraig and there are physical remains of a substantial building there to this day. Their great talents as pipers, handed down through generation after generation, is said to have originally been a magic gift from the fairies, a story motif that occurs elsewhere. In the Islay story of 'The Black Chanter', they are said to have actually stolen the original fairy gift! While arguments as to the absolute truth of the MacCrimmon legend will doubtless continue, the number of stories that have survived about them show how central they have been, and still are, to the Highland bagpipe tradition.

The Black Chanter

Back in the Middle Ages, MacDonald, Lord of the Isles, held court at Finlaggan on Islay. He was effectively the leader of an independent country, having control of the Hebrides and much of the west coast despite the ongoing efforts of the Scottish kings to bring the area under their direct control. It wasn't until 1493 that the Scottish crown destroyed the power-base of the Lords of Isles. Now during this period there was a man at Finlaggan, a ploughman and smith, who was on the big side and was a MacDonald himself. For some reason amongst the Gaels of Scotland, certain Christian names have always been popular and even today there are areas of the Western Isles where several men and boys will have exactly the same name. This has led to a system of nicknames being given and all we now know of the man under consideration is that he was known as the Big Ploughman.

He was a real giant of a man with appetites to match, including an appetite for work. One day he was out ploughing, with a young lad along to help, in the field at Knockshanta (the holy or sacred hill) when a great hunger came on him. Now when the Big Ploughman got hungry the joke in the area was that people used to shut their doors, such was his appetite for food. It was still more than an hour before the time for the midday meal and the Big Ploughman's belly was beginning to rumble. He said to the wee lad, 'I wouldn't care if it came the normal way or by magic but I would take food if it came,' forgetting that the little people are always listening.

Anyway, they took another turn with the horses round the side of Knockshanta and who should be sitting on the side of the wee hill but an old, grey-haired man with a table before him spread with all sorts of grand food.

'Come up and help yourselves lads,' he called out to the two of them.

Such was his hunger the Big Ploughman went up without hesitating but the boy realised this had to be a fairy and wouldn't go. He had heard too many tales of what happened to those foolish enough to eat fairy food – they disappeared, never to be seen again, and it was thought their souls were lost forever. But the Ploughman had no reservations – he was hungry, here was food, he would eat. Once he had eaten – and a goodly amount he put away – he sat back with a contented sigh. At that point the old man handed him a black chanter and said, 'Now give us a tune, lad.'

Now the Ploughman had never shown the least bit of musical ability all his days and certainly did not know how to play the chanter, though he was as fond of a good bit of piping as the next man. Anyway the old man signed him to give it a try so he put the chanter to his lips just as he had seen so many pipers do. As soon as the chanter was on his lips and his fingers fell over the holes the Big Ploughman began to play, and didn't he play just as well as ever any piper in the isle of Islay. He was delighted with this and when the old man gave him the chanter to take away with him he could hardly believe his good fortune.

He lost no time in getting himself a set of bagpipes and fitting the magical chanter to them. Up and down outside his croft he marched playing tune after tune, as if he had been a piper since childhood.

A few days later the MacDonald heard him playing from the castle at Finlaggan and, asking who it was, was told the Big Ploughman. Now the Lord of the Isles was so impressed he ordered the very best set of pipes to be made and gave them to the Big Ploughman, asking him to become the piper at Finlaggan castle. The Ploughman was delighted with his new talents and the idea of a life of relative ease at the castle was not one he found hard to resist at all. No more necessity to get up at the crack of dawn to get the smiddy fire going and no endless hours of back-breaking labour (though truth to tell he had always liked being a smith). But this life would be a lot more enjoyable. He became the piper to the Lord of the Isles and soon everybody on the islands around knew of the great talent of the Big Ploughman of Islay.

A year or two later Macdonald had gone to Skye and came back with a young lad who wanted to learn from the Big Ploughman. This was MacCrimmon, the first of the famous line of pipers, and he was already a fair player. However, he knew he wanted to be a better piper and everyone said to be the best you should learn from the best. Nobody doubted that the Big Ploughman was the best, even if some people had a fair idea that he had got his music from the fairies.

So the young MacCrimmon came to Finlaggan and began to study with the Big Ploughman. Being young, he soon noticed that the daughter of the house was a bonny young lass and began to pay attention to her. She was very taken with the young man from Skye and thought she had found herself a true lover. Soon after arriving, the young man noticed that his teacher was very careful that no-one ever touched his set of pipes. He began to realise that there was something special about the black chanter. He had noticed one day that the Big Ploughman, when he thought he was alone, had picked up MacCrimmon's pipes and given them a blow. The music he made was nowhere near as fine as when he played his own chanter and pipes. This got the young lad thinking, and very carefully he asked around as to where the black chanter had been made. He soon found out that it had been given to the Big Ploughman by the fairies and was the secret of the big man's talent.

So one day he mentioned to the young lass Kirsty that he would really like to have a tune on the black chanter. 'Och, father would go mad if anyone else played his chanter; he has more love for that old thing than even his family,' the young lass replied.

'Och, well,' said MacCrimmon, 'it was just a thought,' pretending he didn't really care one way or the other.

But Kirsty had decided in her heart that the Skye man was the one for her and the attention he had been paying her led her to think he felt the same way. So, after thinking about it a good deal, she told herself: 'Well, he will be marrying me when he gets round to asking, and then he'll be family, so there's no real problem if I let him have a wee tune on the black chanter.'

So one night, after her father was asleep, she crept into his room and got the chanter. She took it to MacCrimmon and they went off a fair distance from the house so he could give it a blow without anyone hearing. As soon as his fingers touched the chanter, didn't they feel like they were on fire. He played every bit as well as the Big Ploughman himself, and in his heart MacCrimmon thought he was even better. After an hour or so Kirsty forced him to give back the chanter and returned it to her father's room. Every night after that MacCrimmon was on at the young lass to get hold of the black chanter; sometimes she would manage to get the chanter to him and sometimes not. Now by this time the Big Ploughman was well aware that there was something going on between Kirsty and MacCrimmon, and he was waiting for the Skye man to come and speak to him about it.

Then word came that MacDonald was heading back to Skye and that he would take MacCrimmon with him. The night before he was to leave, MacCrimmon went on and on at Kirsty to get him the black chanter. She was waiting for him to ask her to marry him. She knew he was going back home, and she thought that if she got him the chanter he would surely ask her after all this time. So she got the chanter and handed it to him.

'Look, Kirsty, I'm going to go and have a last blow on this; as it will be my last chance, I'll bring it back in the morning,' he said. 'Is that all right?'

She looked deep into his eyes and, besotted as she was, she still hoped that at the last he would ask her what she wanted most of all in the world to hear. So she gave him the chanter and he left the Big Ploughman's house.

He didn't return and the last Kirsty saw of him he was standing in the front of MacDonald's birlinn as it was rowed out of Finlaggan harbour. And he was playing his own set of pipes, but with the black chanter. He never did come back to Islay and he never sent for the Big Ploughman's daughter. And this, the Islay men will tell you yet, is how the MacCrimmons took the music to Skye.

MacCrimmon Will Never Return

When Charles Edward Stuart raised his standard at Glenfinnan in 1745 there were people all over the Highlands who thought that things were about to get better. The government in London, even further away than their old adversaries in Edinburgh, had started driving modern metalled roads through the Highlands and the red-coated soldiers could move about the country with ease. The old ways were changing, the clan system was in crisis and the modern money economy was replacing the old subsistence and barter style of life of most Highlanders. The chiefs, traditionally the focus of clan life, were changing too, becoming ever more like landlords, rather than the respected leaders of an integrated kin-based society. People throughout the Highlands were hoping that bringing back the old line of kings would bring back the old certainties and reverse the changes that were tearing their society apart.

Amongst the Highland people nobody was more hopeful than Donald Ban MacCrimmon and his wife. They thought that with a Stewart on the throne their way of life and their culture would be safe. Donald was eager to stand behind the prince and had even composed a sparkling new pibroch in honour of Charles Edward Stuart's arrival. He didn't want to play the tune on the bagpipes till he was part of the prince's army, but he was so pleased with the composition that he sang to it his wife, who agreed it was wonderful piece.

Many of his nearest relations agreed with him that they should be coming out for the prince, but MacCrimmon was hereditary piper to the MacLeod of Dunvegan, and he had other plans. There are those who will tell you that the clan chiefs were men of honour, and those who will tell you that by the eighteenth century many of them were money-grubbing quislings intent on betraying the long-term interests of their kinsmen for their own personal gain. In such matters the facts should be left to speak for themselves. MacLeod had been involved in the scandalous kidnapping and incarceration of Lady Grange, because she had overheard her husband and some of his friends discussing plans to bring the Stewarts back to the throne. He had also been involved in one of the most shameful acts in Scottish history. He and his fellow laird, his brother-in-law MacDonald, Lord of the Isles, had arranged to sell a hundred of their clansmen into slavery in the American plantations. The plan was thwarted when the ship carrying these unfortunate souls was intercepted by the navy and they were all released. It was probably because they were never prosecuted by the government for this despicable act that both MacLeod and MacDonald in the end opted to support the Hanoverian cause.

When they eventually left Skye to join the government troops at Inverness it came as a shock to many of MacLeod's clansmen, but he had given his word and they could not break it. Despite his sore misgivings, MacCrimmon accepted that he would follow his clan chief, but he did so with a heavy heart and a deep sense of foreboding. He would not play the new tune while serving the Hanoverian cause.

MacCrimmon's wife was on the shore at Dunvegan when the clansmen set off in boats for the mainland, aware that her husband thought he was going to his death.

She said later, 'Sad was my heart when from the point I saw the birlinns leave, MacLeod in the stern of the foremost, looking sad and mournful, and MacCrimmon in the prow playing a pibroch – not the joyful pibroch but a sad, sad tune.' This was the tune now known throughout the world as 'Cha Till MacCruimein' – MacCrimmon will never return.

The MacLeods went to Inverness to join Lord Loudon, giving him a substantial force of about 1,600 men. The MacLeods were not long there when the word came from Grant of Delachny, near Moy, that Prince Charlie himself was at Moy Hall, just sixteen miles away. He was there at the invitation of Anne Mackintosh, long known as Colonel Anne for her exploits on behalf of the prince. The Mackintoshes too had problems with which side to be on. The laird of Mackintosh, Anne's husband, had declared for the Hanoverian cause, but Anne was a staunch Jacobite and brought the majority of the clan out for the prince, with one Alexander MacGillivray as clan captain. It is said that she herself rode out on occasion with her clan with a man's bonnet on her head, a tartan riding habit, richly laced, and a pair of pistols in holsters on her saddle. Anne's own father, Farquharson of Invercauld, was also a supporter of the Hanoverian cause. He had 'been out' in support of Prince Charlie's father in 1715 but had decided that discretion was the better part of valour and had gone over to support the Hanoverian monarchs. However, Anne's mother-in-law the Dowager Lady Mackintosh was, like Anne, a fervent Jacobite. She was living in her house in Inverness when the MacLeods arrived and, as her son was known to be a government man, she was under no suspicion. Loudon, having been tipped off by Grant of Delachny, thought he would simply go out and capture the prince, thus putting an end to the entire rebellion. That would sort things out pretty quickly, he thought. Although the town was sealed and under tight security, a serving lass in a local tavern who happened to be a Mackintosh over-heard plans being laid for the march to Moy. She informed the Dowager Lady Mackintosh. Lachlan Mackintosh, who was working in Lady Mackintosh's house in Inverness, was sent to take word to Colonel Anne.

The young lad set out on the road to Moy, only to find that ahead of him was a detachment of MacLeods. Behind him he could hear another group approaching, which would have been Lord Loudon's regiment. He was trapped! Aware that being out at night on the road to Moy, and a Mackintosh, he was liable to be arrested, the young lad dived into a ditch and lay there silently until the last of the troops passed. As soon as they had passed he was out of the ditch and off into the hills. He knew the area like the back of his hand, was a fit young lad and could travel faster on his own than a large body of troops could hope to do. So he headed up and along the sides of Beinn Bhreac and was soon ahead of the troops. As he ran, the heavens opened and lightning flashed as a thunderstorm rolled into the hills.

He reached Moy Hall in the middle of the night, pouring with sweat, and raised the household to tell them the news that the government troops were close behind him. The prince set off east along Moy Loch to meet with Lochiel, who had five hundred men with him. They would be outnumbered if Loudon caught them up, but the prince was resolved to make a fight of it. However, no one had realised just how capable Colonel Anne was. She was unsure of the loyalty of Grant of Delachny and suspected he might send word of the prince's presence at Moy. So, at sundown the previous day, she had sent the local black-smith, a Fraser, and five other men along the road to Inverness with muskets. They had hidden on the moor overnight in a hollow called 'ciste chraig nan coin' and had seen nothing of Lachlan, who had come in along the mountainside. Just as Colonel Anne was gathering more men to come to their assistance and delay the government's advance, the MacLeods were approaching Fraser and his small band. Seeing them come, he spread his men out in a line, and told them to wait till he fired.

At the head of the MacLeod troops was Donald MacCrimmon himself, in the traditional leading position. His pipes were tucked under his arm ready, but he was under orders not to play till they were close to Moy Hall. A shot rang out and MacCrimmon fell. More shots were fired and Fraser and his men began shouting the Cameron and MacDonald war cries and calling, 'They have come for our prince; attack, attack!'

MacLeod of Dunvegan immediately thought that he was faced by a large body of troops from several clans and halted his men. With the pouring rain, the thunder and the flashes of lightning and muskets the situation appeared chaotic. Out there in the open he thought that the enemy were well entrenched and called for a retreat. At that point, a MacDonald who was with the MacLeods and a cousin of MacCrimmon's wife crept forward to see how the piper was. As he approached, he heard MacCrimmon strike up a tune. Lying there on his back in the heather, with the life-blood pouring from a great hole in his side, Donald Ban was playing a bright and lively tune that MacDonald had never heard before. The great piper played on till he had not a breath left in his body and died there in the heather.

Meanwhile Fraser, known ever after as Captein nan Coig – Captain of the Five – kept up the shooting and the shouting while the very rattled MacLeod led his and Loudon's men away from the moor. The prince met up with Lochiel and by the time they returned to Moy Hall the government troops were well on their way back to the fortifications at Inverness. They had been routed by five men and the only casualty of the engagement was Donald Ban MacCrimmon. The incident has been known as the Rout of Moy ever since.

Months later, MacDonald got back to Dunvegan and went to see Donald Ban's widow. He told her of what had happened and when he came to the bit about the last tune he was playing, she asked him to sing it. Though no piper, he could carry a tune, and the bright sparking notes he had heard that fateful day at Moy had stuck in his memory. So he sang the tune and at once she recognised it as the tune MacCrimmon had composed when he thought he was going off to join the prince. Many years later, as an old woman, she told the story, and said that MacCrimmon had heard the banshee, the spirit that forewarns of death, before he left Skye that last time. This was why he had composed 'Cha Till MacCruimen', and maybe why that tune is still remembered. What the other tune was no one now knows.

The Stolen Tune

Once a great piping contest was to be held at Dunvegan. Pipers from all over the Highlands and Islands of Scotland were coming to Skye for the event and it was expected that whoever won this competition would be crowned king of the pipers by his fellow musicians. At the time one of the MacCrimmon pipers had a pupil who was his nephew, of whom he expected great things. The lad had a great style, a tremendous ear for music, was a hard worker and always seemed ready to do whatever his uncle told him. He was obviously destined to be a very fine piper and his uncle was very fond of him. When the competition was announced the uncle determined to win it. He would be pleased to get the first prize, which was a set of brand new pipes chased in silver, but what mattered most was the winning – it would be a great thing to be known as the finest piper of all.

Now he had been teaching his nephew for quite a few years by this time and such was his devotion to the young lad that he had taught him everything he knew. All of his years of playing and learning had been passed on to the young lad. All except one thing. On the quiet, the elder piper had been composing a new tune, with which he hoped to win the competition. He had never let his nephew hear it for he knew that even with one hearing the lad would be able to get the piece, such was his musical ability. So the uncle had been forced to practice the piece in secret, away from his young pupil. However, the young lad had sensed something was up, though he had no idea what it was.

The great day came and the pair of them set out for Dunvegan from their home on the mainland. It was a fair journey and they had to stop overnight at an inn. In those days Highland inns were not the outstanding examples of comfort and hospitality that they are (well, some of them) today. They were rough and ready bothies and it was in no way unusual for men to share a bed in such places. So they got a room and climbed in opposite sides of the bed.

After a little while, the elder piper, thinking his nephew was sound asleep, began humming the new tune to himself very quietly. The nephew turned over in his sleep and flung an arm across his uncle, who was lying on his back. At this point the uncle was getting a bit drowsy and, without thinking, began to lightly finger the tune on his nephew's arm. The lad was awake in an instant but did not move a muscle. As soon as he was awake he was aware of what was going on. He realised that the tune being fingered on his arm was one he had never heard played. This must be what his uncle had been doing when he went off on his own – he had been practising a new tune for the competition. The older man fingered through the tune three times before he fell into a deep sleep. By that point his talented young nephew had the tune off pat.

The following day the nephew said nothing as they went on their way to Dunvegan Castle. He had listened to his uncle when he had said, 'I have taught you all I know; now, lad, it is up to you to become a better piper by yourself, if you can.' He had taken his uncle at his word and felt a wee bit betrayed that the older man had an extra tune prepared for the competition. He realised that he was still young and inexperienced but had thought that he might have a chance of winning the competition. After all, his uncle was reckoned to be one of the best pipers in the land and he had often given him compliments such as, 'Well lad, you'll have the beating of me yet,' or, 'One day, lad, you will be one of the very best, and better than myself.' But the poor uncle wasn't looking forward to that particular day at all.

They came at last to Dunvegan Castle and there was such a gathering of pipers as had been rarely seen before. Some had come from other islands, many from the Highlands, and a goodly crowd had come from even further south: Glasgow, Edinburgh and even the Borders. The nephew noticed that his uncle knew a great many of the pipers and that they all treated him with respect. Listening intently to his elders, he found out that his uncle was surely one of the favourites to take the prize. 'Especially,' he thought, 'if he has a brand new tune for the occasion.'

One by one the pipers registered for the competition; when the nephew followed his uncle, the elder man said, 'Ach, just you go before me.' All at once his heart was in his mouth. He could play the new tune! Or could he? Would this not be a betrayal of the trust between teacher and pupil? But he was young, and remembered that the new tune had been kept a secret from him. Right up till the moment of starting to play he was unsure what to do, but as soon as he was announced to the gathered crowd and walked onto the stage, he knew what he must do.

His uncle's face when he heard his nephew begin to play was a sight to see. His plans were ruined. The lad played the tune and played it brilliantly. He played it so well that he was cheered to the echo and his uncle knew that he would not be able to play it any better. For the first time he realised that his nephew was no longer going to become a better player than he was; that time had already come. So, with a sad acceptance, he too played the new tune, knowing in his heart that he would not outclass the young lad. The outcome was clear and the nephew won the competition. From that day on he was no longer his uncle's pupil, but a first-class piper in his own right – and a competition winner!

A Grand Pair of Lungs!

Nowadays there are pipers who have learned circular breathing as a technique to improve their playing but in the past it was considered good enough to practise regularly. It has long been known that piping is good for the lungs and that pipers are never bothered with weak chests. However, some pipers can certainly be said to have had remarkable lung power. One of these was Finlay MacCrimmon, known as Finlay of the White Plaid. The plaid is the traditional one-piece garment of the Highland people and consists of a length of woollen cloth several yards long. Men wore it kilted round the waist with a belt, with the rest of it thrown over the shoulders or hanging down at the back. The plaid was of course a remarkably versatile garment and warriors would wrap themselves up in it to sleep out on the hills. In the winter they would even go as far as to soak their plaids in water before wrapping themselves in them and lying down to sleep. It is one of wool's most remarkable properties that it retains more heat when it is wet than when it is dry. The tartan patterns, nowadays associated with specific clans, were originally much more widespread and were more associated with a particular area rather than one specific clan. This was because they were created from what local dying materials were available, so particular tartans would often spread across considerable areas. The standard way of identifying clan warriors was in fact by the clan plant, a sprig of which was usually affixed to the warrior's bonnet.

The plaids were almost universally worn. Finlay MacCrimmon, however, decided that he didn't want to wear tartan and had his plaid spun out of white wool. His fame as a piper was probably eclipsed by this sartorial eccentricity. Finlay was also a great warrior; on one occasion he took on a dozen other men. This group had been behaving like bandits and Finlay decided to sort them out. Although they were all Highland warriors too, Finlay ended up triumphant. Those he didn't kill he tied up with fishing line and marched to Dunvegan Castle to be dealt with by the MacLeod. He was, in short, a remarkable man.

One time he was out fishing at night on Loch Dunvegan with four men from Clan McLeod. It was one of those nights when the mist was blowing in and out of the loch; through the swirling banks of cloud, Finlay caught sight of a group of birlinns entering the loch. Coming in at night was hardly the action of a friend and Finlay at once realised that this was a raid to attack Dunvegan Castle itself, or the rich farmland around it. Like the incoming force, Finlay and his companions were in a birlinn, the traditional oar-driven boat of the west of Scotland. However, with only five rowers they were not best equipped to get up much speed – the birlinns normally carried around a dozen men. Still, they had to get ashore to raise the alarm, so they set to with all their strength.

Soon, however, they were spotted by the incoming marauders, who gave chase. With fully-manned birlinns they could make much greater speed and by the time Finlay made the shore the raiders were upon them. There was a short fight, in which all of the four MacLeods were killed. Finlay killed two or three of the incomers and ran off. Past the clachan of Galtrigill he ran. He kept running till he was on Dunvegan Head. As he reached the highpoint overlooking the sea he was totally enveloped in the mist that was swirling about at sea level. There was no point in even trying to light a beacon fire. Finlay knew what he must do. He stood still and began to breathe slowly. As his heart slowed down and he began to feel a little calmer he took in a great breath of air. He then blew it out and breathed in again. Again he breathed out. And again he sucked in as much air as he could. Facing towards the clan stronghold of Dunvegan Castle, fully seven miles away down the loch, Finlay of the White Plaid let out a mighty roar. He knew there was little chance of words carrying that far, but the sound of his voice might. Twice more he breathed his lungs full of air and let out bull-like roars.

Seven miles away on the battlements of the castle, the watchman on duty heard the three great bull-roars coming down the loch. Immediately he ran to wake the chief and sound the alarm. Within minutes a couple of dozen fully-armed men were on the battlements; others were summoned to man the birlinns down on the shore. The marauders on the loch had heard the three roars, but carried on towards Dunvegan. As the mist swirled, they saw the castle all lit up, and half a dozen birlinns heading out towards them. They turned and fled, chased far away from

Skye by the pursuing MacLeods. The piper's lungs had saved the
day. Or perhaps one should say the MacCrimmons fair could blaw!

Squinting Patrick

Donald Mor MacCrimmon's brother lived at Glenelg, opposite
Skye – a place long associated with heroes. He was called Peter
Caog, Squinting Peter, because of a problem in one eye, which
caused it to look the other way from where he intended. Back in
the times when all male Highlanders were warriors they lived by
a strict code of honour, but bad blood can always arise between
people. Now Peter Caog had had a quarrel with his foster
brother, a Mackenzie from Kintail. Foster brothers were raised
together just like blood brothers and when such close relation-
ships founder there are often dreadful consequences. The quarrel
was allowed to fester. One day when Peter was in the hills of
Kintail he stopped to take a drink from a burn. Unknown to him,
his foster brother had been on his trail all day. Seizing his chance,
he crept up on the kneeling MacCrimmon and dirked him as he
drank. Peter died instantly.

When Donald Mor heard of this treachery his sadness at his
brother's death was outweighed by the anger he felt towards
Mackenzie. This evil deed called for revenge. In order to do
things right he couldn't just run off to find Mackenzie and kill
him. He went to Dunvegan Castle and asked where MacLeod
was. Being told he was in his bedroom, MacCrimmon marched
straight in and threw his pipes on the chief's bed.

'I demand revenge on Mackenzie for the murder of my
brother,' he hissed. MacLeod had a high opinion of Donald Ban
and realised that by throwing his pipes onto the bed he was
reminding him of his position as clan piper and asking for due
consideration in this dreadful matter. However, MacLeod was a
canny man and replied, 'It shall be done within the year, Donald
Ban, never fear.'

In saying this MacLeod was hoping that within a year Donald would calm down and perhaps another way could be found to address the situation. He was concerned that starting a blood feud with the Mackenzies would be a dangerous course of action. However, there was no doubt that Donald Ban had a case and, when at the end of the year MacLeod had done nothing, he resolved to take matters into his own hands.

Donald went alone to Glenelg, to the clachan where Mackenzie lived, and asked for him to be handed over as a murderer. The Mackenzies refused to hand him over. They had in fact sent the culprit off into the hills when word came that MacLeod's piper had come from Dunvegan to Glenelg, as no one was in any doubt as to what Donald had in mind.

'So you will not hand him over to me,' said Donald, as calm as you like. 'Well, on your own heads be it.'

This was clearly a threat and some of the Mackenzies would have liked to have killed MacCrimmon there and then, but wiser heads realised that this would be foolish. To kill the famous piper of the MacLeods would undoubtedly bring the whole clan down upon them. So Donald left the clachan in Glenelg. But he did not go far, not far at all.

He headed off back in the direction of Skye, but as soon as he was out of sight of the clachan he headed into the hills to await nightfall. His anger and desire for justice had been smouldering away for a year and had been getting stronger all the time. To Donald Ban it was not revenge he was seeking but justice itself. Mackenzie had murdered his brother in cold blood and no one had raised a hand against him. The insult ran deep, as did the loss he felt for his brother. So he sat out in the hills till night fell.

Like all Highlandmen of his time, Donald was a skilled warrior and he laid his plans carefully as he sat in the heather out of sight of the clachan. He had made sure that none of the Mackenzies had followed him. They would be thinking he was well on his way back to Dunvegan by now. The first that knew was when cries of 'Fire! Fire!' echoed through the glen.

Men grabbed their weapons and ran outside; women gathered up their children and followed, for the black houses of the time, with their thatches of heather, could catch light in seconds from blown sparks. As the Mackenzies stumbled out into the centre of the clachan they realised that eighteen houses were ablaze. Donald Ban had crept silently down and gone about his dreadful work in absolute silence. As the distraught families of the clachan began to try to fight the fire they heard a sound. They could hear bagpipes playing! It was Donald Ban MacCrimmon, standing on a nearby crag overlooking the clachan, playing a wild and furious tune that no one had ever heard before. This was 'Lasan Phadruig Chaoig' – 'A Flame of Wrath for Squinting Peter'.

Some of the men immediately went after Donald but, long before they got to where he was playing, he had finished the tune and disappeared into the night.

Now, because his own chief had not intervened, Donald was on his own. He had consulted no one and had acted alone. The chief of the Mackenzies would hear soon enough and he realised that the hunt would be up for him. He would not even be safe at home, as the Mackenzie would come to MacLeod of Dunvegan himself. His action in firing the entire clachan had clearly been beyond the pale. So Donald went off into the hills opposite Skye, where he had a close friend in a shepherd who lived high in the hills.

Mackenzie soon heard where Donald Ban was hiding and sent out a group of twelve men to capture him. It was a typically wet west-coast day and by the time the men reached the shepherd's house they were soaking. Because of the heavy rain, the shepherd's wife had only seen them coming at the last minute. She ordered Donald into the bed at far side of the house from the fire, where he hid under the blankets.

At this time the standard male Highland dress was still the belted plaid – even though they were warmer when wet, plaids retained a lot of water, which made them heavy, so wearing them in the rain was a bit uncomfortable. As soon as the Mackenzies got to the door, the lady of the house ushered them in, saying, 'Och, it's a right wet day, so come on in lads and dry off your plaids.' This they proceeded to do before searching the house; as they undid their plaids they stood around the fire in their long shirts. As each plaid came off, the wily woman hung them up between the fire and the bed where Donald was lying still. Within a few minutes there was enough cover for him to slide from the bed and sneak out into the rain.

On being asked where Donald Ban MacCrimmon was by the leader of the group, the chief's eldest son Ewan, the shepherd's wife could honestly reply that she didn't know. She did know where he had been, but that was not what she was asked. So the house was searched and not a trace of Donald found. At this point, with the rain still streaming down, the lady of the house asked Ewan if he would like a dram and the old whisky flagon was brought out. By the time her husband came back from the hill they were all well settled in for the night. The men would sleep on the floor, but she insisted on making up a proper bed for Ewan, just by the door. They all stretched out with their weapons handily placed against the walls of the tigh dubh (black house).

In the middle of the night, when all were sound asleep, the whisky making sure they would notice nothing, Donald Ban came into the house. Very carefully he took swords, pistols, dirks and a musket or two and placed them over the sleeping Ewan.

In the morning the young chieftain awoke to find himself in what seemed to be a cage of weapons. Shoving them aside, he roared at his clansmen, 'I might have been killed for all the help you were. Donald Mor has been in this house in the night and it would have been easy for him to have taken my life as I slept.' There were more than a few hang-dog looks and sheepish expressions as the Mackenzies realised they had been made to look like fools.

On going outside, who should they see standing on the other side of the burn but Donald Mor, sword and targe in hand. A couple of the Mackenzies grabbed their own weapons and made as if to go for Donald.

Then came a loud command: 'I will shoot the first man to try to cross that burn.' It was Ewan himself.

'Will you come over this side of the burn, Donald Mor? I give my pledge of honour you shall not be injured,' he called out.

'Will your companions give me their pledge too?' Donald called back. At this there were a few mutterings but, under the instruction of their chief's son, one after the other the Mackenzies gave their pledge that Donald would not be harmed.

So he came over and stood before Ewan Mackenzie.

'Well, Donald Ban MacCrimmon, was it you who piled the arms over me in the night?' he asked.

'Aye, I did that,' replied the piper.

'You might just as easily have killed me,' said Ewan, watching Donald closely.

The piper smiled but said nothing.

'I will tell you what I will do. Because of this I will secure you a pardon if you will come to my father's house three weeks from today. Will you do that?' he asked.

'I will,' replied Donald, and the two men shook hands.

So it was agreed, and Donald Ban went back to Dunvegan. Three weeks later he returned to Glenelg. On his way to the chief's home on the appointed day he stopped at the house of Mackenzie's fiddler, a two-storeyed building, rare at the time. The musicians knew each other well but the fiddler, a Mackay, had been away from the glen to visit his own people and did not know that the chief's son had secured a pardon from his father for Donald Ban. He thought that Donald Ban was still being sought for the burning of the clachan. He invited him in and showed him into the house, taking him upstairs into a room, saying he would be with him in a minute. Going downstairs, the fiddler sent one of his children to gather up as many men as he could and bring them to the house to capture Donald Ban.

Luckily for Donald, Ewan Mackenzie's younger brother had been in the house having a fiddle lesson when he arrived. After a few minutes, the fiddler came back upstairs and asked Donald to come down for a dram or two.

'Aye, fine,' said Donald, and opened the door. There with the fiddler was the chief's younger son, who whispered that it was a trap. All at once Donald Ban grabbed the fiddler, threw him down the stairs and retreated into the room, locking the door behind him. The younger son ran off to fetch his brother. While the fiddler and the gathered men were still discussing how to get Donald out of the upstairs room with as little trouble as possible, Ewan Mackenzie arrived, running to tell them all that his father had pardoned Donald, and that the killer of Patrick Coag would be tried for murder. Once things were cleared up, both Mackay and MacCrimmon went to the Mackenzie's castle and that night they all had a bit of a ceilidh. Donald's persistence had paid off.

The First MacCrimmon

The following story is taken from a manuscript written in 1651 by James Fraser, minister of Wardlaw near Beauly. Charles II had been crowned at Scone on New Year's Day 1651. Two years earlier, the English parliament under the control of English independents led by Oliver Cromwell had executed his father Charles I. This broke the alliance that had been formed between the Independents and the Presbyterians in Scotland. The Scottish Covenanters had rallied behind Charles, who signed the Solemn League and Covenant supporting Presbyterianism in June 1650; he was then endorsed by the Scottish parliament. His greatest supporter, the duke of Montrose, had been captured and was executed in May of that year. Severe defeats followed for the

Scottish forces and the country was in turmoil. It was against this background that Fraser tells of the march of the Frasers, four hundred of them, to join up with their new king at Stirling. It was towards the end of April when they came down from Inverness through Badenoch and Appin, arriving at the king's camp at the beginning of May. The king himself was delighted at the spectacle of these Highland warriors and called them the flower of his forces, telling all who would listen how highly he thought of them. In typical Stewart fashion he seemed unaware of the resentment this caused amongst his Lowland officers and their men. Despite the seriousness of the situation in which they found themselves, the army still had some time for entertainment. Following a competition amongst the trumpeters – won, on the king's judgement, by a man called Axell, who was trumpeter to the earl of Home – a competition was held amongst the pipers. As Fraser tells it, there really was no competition at all. None of the pipers was prepared to compete against John MacGrumen, the earl of Sutherland's piper, who, unopposed, won. A day or two later the king was reviewing all his troops when he noticed that there was a separate group of pipers, all bare-headed, except one standing in their midst. He asked what was going on and was told, 'Sir, you are our king and the old man in the middle of the crowd is the prince of pipers.' Being told his name, he called MacGrumen over; the old man came and knelt before the king. At this point Charles put out his hand for the piper to kiss. As soon as he had done so, MacGrumen skirled up his pipe and extemporised a new tune on the spot.

He called the tune 'Thuair Mi Pog o' Laimh An Righ', 'I Got a Kiss of the King's Hand'. Campsie says in his critique of the MacCrimmons that there is no certainty that this is the same tune as the one known by that name since the early nineteenth century. However, there is no certainty that it isn't either. The royalist army then headed into England and at Worcester on 3 September met their final defeat.

The Black Lad MacCrimmon and the Banshee

Now it is well known that fairies and other types of spirits loved music and there were often good players among them. In the Highlands most of these magical creatures played the bagpipes and it was the quality of their music, no doubt, that led to the stories of people being lured into fairy mounds for what seemed a night but turned out to be a hundred years or more. Now and again one of these otherworldly creatures would take a human under his wing and give him the fairy skill at music. Up till the time of the MacCrimmon known as the Black Lad, his family were no better than any other decent pipers in Scotland. Sure, some of them were pipers and some were not, but what happened to the Black Lad changed all that for ever.

Now the Black Lad, 'an Ghille Dubh', was the youngest of three sons and the least thought-of by his father. They all lived together on Skye. His father would take the crooked stick of the great bagpipes which he called the Black Gate from behind the door, and he himself would play. He was happy to let his two eldest sons play on his pipes but the third son, the Black Lad, was not considered worth such an honour and wouldn't even get a blow on the pipes. He was generally badly treated and treated as little more than a slave by his father and brothers. One day the three of them went off to a nearby fair, leaving the Black Lad on his own. He was a bright lad, despite what his family thought, and had been learning the chanter on the sly, mainly by observing his father and brothers when they played, and listening closely. So that day, thinking he was alone, he took the chanter from his father's pipes and struck up a tune. He was sitting there happily playing away on the chanter when who should come upon him but the banshee who looked after the MacLeods. As the MacCrimmons were a sept of that clan, the banshee was watching over them as well. Now, usually, people only heard the banshee when she cried out to forewarn of imminent death or disaster to the clan, but she was always about, if unseen.

So the Black Lad is there concentrating on his fingering when suddenly this female sprite appears before him.

'Playing music, then, are we?' she asked and the young fellow was so surprised he just answered straight off, 'Aye, I am that.' He was so surprised that he didn't have time to be frightened of this spectral being, though he immediately knew who she was.

'Well then, lad, would you rather have skill without success or success without skill?' she asked him, her head on one side and looking at him from under her bushy eyebrows.

'Skill without success,' he answered back with no hesitation at all.

'Skill without success. Well then,' she said, 'let's just see.'

And she pulled a hair from her hoary old head and asked him to tie it round the reed of the chanter and when that was done she told him, 'Now take the chanter in your hands and I will lay my fingers on thy fingers.'

So they did.

'Now, when I lift my finger, lift thou the one that happens to be underneath it. Think of any tune you like and play it along with me.'

He did just that and played the tune with great skill. When he finished the tune he just sat there looking from the chanter to the banshee and back again – surely he couldn't have played that!

Then the banshee said to him, 'Now thou art the king of the pipers. Thine equal was not before thee, and thine equal shall not come after thee.'

Just as soon as she had said that, she was gone. Filled with amazement and happiness, he got down the Black Gate from behind the door and started to play. There was not a tune he could think of but he could play it right away almost without thinking. So on and on he played, unaware of time passing till his father and brothers were getting back home from the fair. They had had a drop or two of whisky and were humming and singing tunes to each other as they came along the road.

As they came near to their house they heard this wonderful music being played and stopped to listen.

'Whoever that great piper is he's playing on the Black Gate,' said the father. 'I would recognise the sound of my own pipes anywhere. Come lads, let's see who it is.' And they hurried to see who was playing. But just before they got to the house the music ceased. They looked at each other and said not a word. A suspicion was forming in their minds and when they came into the cottage to find the Black Lad sitting alone by the fire, they said not a word, but exchanged meaningful glances.

Later that night the father took down the Black Gate from behind the door and this time, after he and his two eldest sons had played, he turned to the Black Lad. 'Now you play,' he said.

'But I am not worthy of the honour; I am happy as I am,' the young man replied. 'Do as you are told and take the bagpipes,' said his father, 'and we'll all start mucking in about the place from now on,' he went on with a smile on his face.

So the Black Lad played in front of his family for the very first time and wasn't he better than any of them, and better than anyone else they had ever heard before.

'The music has left us,' said the father to his two other sons. 'None of us will come in the wake of the Black Lad.'

And he spoke the truth for never before or since has there been a piper who could play as well as the Black Lad.

A Different Way of Telling the Same Story

Now it is in the way of things that the same stories are told in many different places. In some cases, though the stories are similar and mean the same thing, they are very much localised versions. People always tended to tell their stories within an environment that their audience would recognise, so it is little wonder that there are many areas that lay claim to stories concerning the MacCrimmons.

It is said that at one time on Skye there was a famous MacCrimmon piper. He had three sons and MacCrimmon reckoned that the two eldest of his boys were good pipers and could be trusted to keep up the family tradition of piping. The third son, however, was a different case. They called him Daft Donald and he wasn't maybe quite as bright as his brothers. He was left pretty much to his own devices and had got himself an old set of pipes his father had laid aside. After he had done his various chores about the place, he used to play away to himself at the far end of the big long house that his father had, well away from his father and brothers. His father didn't think it worth his time trying to teach Donald to improve his skills; he was quite happy that two of his sons were following in his footsteps and, truth to tell, was disappointed in his third son, though he did try to hide the fact.

One day a couple of pipers came to Skye from Howbeg in South Uist. They had heard of the great skill of MacCrimmon and had come to challenge him to a piping competition.

When they came to MacCrimmon's big long house they were made welcome. The two of them and MacCrimmon and his three sons sat in the main room of the house and the father said, 'Well, seeing as you have come all this way and you have challenged me, I think it only right and proper that one of you should play first.'

Now this did not suit the South Uist lads, who wanted to hear what they were up against, so they had to try and avoid starting things off.

'Och no, haven't we been hearing all about your great skill as a piper?' said one of them. 'And we would think it ill to go before a man with your reputation.'

This is just the way things went, each party trying to gain the advantage over the other. Well, after a while it was clear that things weren't going to be settled in a hurry, so MacCrimmon decided that they would need something to wet their whistles while they hammered out how the competition would be organised.

'Donald,' he said, 'here's some silver; now you run off to Torquil's and bring us back a wee keg of whisky.'

This suggestion was welcomed by the South Uist men and Donald went off down the glen to get some whisky from Torquil, who lived a mile and a bit over the hill. On the way to Torquil's croft he had to pass a wee hill that people said was a fairy hill. As he came up to it who should be sitting on it but a big old man with a great grey beard covering all of his chest.

'Hello Donald,' he said, as the young lad came along the path beside the fairy hill. Now Donald may not have been the brightest star in the sky, but he realised that this old man who knew his name had to be a fairy, and he knew that you had to be careful of the fairies. You never knew what mischief they had planned, so it was always the best bet to steer as clear of them as you could. Still, the man had spoken to him; he obviously knew who he was and it would be impolite not to answer. If you were impolite to a fairy he could get in the mood for mischief pretty quick.

'Good day, to you,' replied Donald, wanting to get on his way as quickly as he could.

'Now, now, Donald, don't be in such a hurry. I know fine well where you are going,' the old man said with a chuckle. 'You're off to Torquil's for a keg of whisky.'

Donald looked a bit apprehensive so the old man chuckled again and said, 'Och, don't you be feart now Donald; I mean you no harm. In fact I want to do you a wee favour before you go and get the whisky.'

'And what would that be?' asked Donald, not at all reassured by the fairy's words.

50

'Well, I know about the Howbeg pipers and I also know from my cousins over there in South Uist that they are very fine pipers indeed.'

'Ay,' said Donald, 'and what has that got to do with me?'

Again the fairy laughed. 'Right, Donald, if you do as I tell you we will make sure that the Howbeg pipers do not show up the MacCrimmons on Skye. Now, I want you to put your fingers, all of them, directly over my fingers; then I want you to stick your tongue in my mouth. Don't be feart, for once you have done this you will be a fine piper and there won't be a piper anywhere in the world that can match you. What do you say?' And the old fairy stood there grinning like a madman at Donald.

Now Donald wished nothing more than to be a fine piper. He wanted to make his father as proud of him as he was of his two elder brothers and though he couldn't be sure that this wasn't a fairy trick, he reckoned it was worth the risk if he could get his father to look on him with pride.

So he did as the fairy told him: he put his fingers over the fairy's fingers then got real close and stuck his tongue in the fairy's mouth. It wasn't a pleasant sensation but it was over in an instant. Then the fairy stood back and began speaking.

'Now go and get yourself the whisky from Torquil. When you get back to your father's house they will still be arguing as to who should go first, even after they have a dram of the whisky you'll be bringing. So, as they argue, just you say "I'll play first." Now your father and your two brothers will tell you not to; in fact they will insist, but never you mind what they say. Just you go and get that old set of pipes you have at the far end of the house and play a tune on them. As soon as the Uist men hear you they will be off, believe you me. Now run and get your whisky.'

Donald went off at a fair lick, but after a hundred yards or so he turned round; he was feeling a bit out of his depth and thought he should maybe go back and have a few more words with the fairy. But there was no sign of the greybeard, so he went on to fetch the whisky.

Now, when he got back with the new keg of whisky, his father and the two visitors had been drinking the bottle that had been in the house, but they still hadn't settled who was to play first.

Donald put down the wee whisky keg and said straight out, 'Ach, you lot are right sticky. I tell you what, I'll play.' And before either his father or brothers could say a word he went to the far end of the house and came back with the old raggedy set of pipes he played on.

As he got back, his father stood up and said, 'Now, Donald, enough. We'll have none of your caterwauling here.'

But Donald got the bag under his oxter, put the mouthpiece in his mouth and began to blow up the bag.

'For heaven's sake, Donald,' shouted his elder brother. 'Don't you start with that racket in front of our guests.'

The second brother chipped in: 'Donald, do as you're told and put those pipes away, now this very minute.'

But Donald had decided to take the old fairy's advice and struck up a tune. Now the pipes he was playing were an old and tattered set and had a tendency for the drones to go right out of tune. His father and his brothers were aghast; they were just waiting for some horrible skraichs and squeaks to come whirling out of the old pipes. Then Donald started, and within three notes his father and two brothers were gaping at each other. How could this be? What was going on? Daft Donald was playing superbly. Up and down the room he marched, playing an old battle tune. The rest of the company just stared.

The two men from Howbeg looked at each other and knew what the other was thinking: if this was the worst of them, they had no chance of beating any of the MacCrimmons. This daft laddie was a far better piper than either of them. What must his brothers and father be like? As soon as Donald finished, with his father and brothers sitting there stunned, the South Uist lads made their excuses and left. From that time on nobody ever made Daft Donald MacCrimmon play at the far end of his father's house. Or any other house.

The MacCrimmons' Silver Chanter

One day in Skye Iain Og MacCrimmon, one of the very first MacCrimmons to take to the pipes, was sitting sadly on a mound near the family home at Boreraig in Skye. He was disappointed that he had not been invited to participate in a piping competition that was taking place at nearby Dunvegan Castle, ancestral home of the MacLeods. The prize was to become the hereditary piper to MacLeod of MacLeod at the castle. His playing had let him down. He let out a deep sigh, which was heard by a fairy living nearby in a fairy mound. The fairy knew Iain Og was a pretty good piper, and he knew of course that Iain had a sweetheart amongst his fairy kin, who had first noticed him because of the sweetness of his way with the pipes. These romances were rare enough and were treasured by human and fairy alike. The fairy could not bear to see Iain so sad and like all of his kind, the elfin creature had a way of knowing things without being told. So he approached the disconsolate young piper and said to him, 'Your manly good looks and the sweetness of your music have brought you a fairy sweetheart. Now I give you this silver chanter, which at the merest touch of your fingers will forever bring the sweetest music from the pipes. But know this, Iain Og, we never give gifts lightly and if you, or any of your descendants, do not treat this chanter with due consideration and respect, the gift of the piping will go from amongst you. Be sure to tell your sons and that they in turn tell their sons.'

Amazed at his good luck and aware of the great gift he was being given, Iain could only stammer out a few words of thanks before the fairy melted away in front of his eyes and returned to his home in the mound. At once Iain fitted the chanter to his pipes and, as soon as he started playing, his sadness departed, for with the magic chanter of the fairies came total command over the playing of pibrochs. He thought for a moment then made up his mind. Straight away he headed back to Dunvegan, where the competition was still going on. When he came to within a mile of the castle he began to play, and when the judges heard him coming they realised that this piper was well worthy of entering the competition. So he was given the chance to play with all the rest and there was no doubt in the minds of anyone who heard him there. He was far and away the best piper that day at Dunvegan. Steeped as they all were in the knowledge of their ancestors, many of those present that day, especially the older pipers who were judging, realised that this young piper had been blessed with the fairy gift of music and that no mere human could hope to match him. And this is how, it is said, that Iain Og became the first of the MacCrimmons to be piper to the MacLeods. From him came many generations of gifted and skilful pipers.

It was many generations later that the MacCrimmon piper was coming back in the MacLeod's birlinn from a journey to the nearby island of Raasay. The wind was picking up and a swell rising on the sea. Perched at the front of the boat in the traditional piper's seat, as usual, MacCrimmon was being moved about to such an extent that he was having some trouble playing. His skilful fingers, practised through many years at playing the ceol mor, slipped from the odd note as the swell built up and he was forced to move to keep his balance. He became increasingly annoyed as more and more notes were played badly or even missed entirely. He was a MacCrimmon, hereditary piper of the clan MacLeod and was affronted that the rest of the men in the birlinn could hear how badly he was playing. One or two of them started making comments about how badly he was playing, one even going as far as saying, 'Och, a woman could do better.'

Another one added, 'Come on MacCrimmon, can you not do better than that?' Embarrassed and angry, MacCrimmon took the mouthpiece from his lips and, unthinking, uttered the fateful words, 'It's this damned chanter . . .'

As soon as the words left his lips, he knew he had made an awful mistake. However, there was nothing at all he could do as he saw the ancient silver chanter, the gift of the fairies to his long-dead ancestor, detach itself from the pipes and float up from the boat, over the gunwale and into the sea, where they say it lies to this day.

With the careless loss of the silver chanter the MacCrimmons were no better than any other good pipers and their long supremacy just faded away. It is said that the school of piping that is reputed to have existed at Boreraig in those days soon closed its doors. The time of the MacCrimmons was over and it has been many a year since any of them owned even a scrap of land in Skye, where once they were supreme.

The Silver Chanter 2

A long time ago a young lad called MacCrimmon wanted to learn the pipes. Try as hard as he could, he was never much use. He heard lots of pipers and tried to emulate their music on an old set of pipes that his father had managed to find for him. But no matter how hard he tried he couldn't seem to master the instrument. One day his father had gone off with his brothers to a local fair and Iain was left behind on his own. He went for a walk down to the shore, carrying the chanter from the old set of pipes, and all the time he was thinking how much he would have liked to go to the fair. Fairs were always interesting and he thought of the bustle of activity round the cattle pens, the stalls selling all sorts of goods, particularly shoes, for he was in sore need of a new pair himself. Then he thought of the food being sold, particularly the sweetmeats and honey and how much he would like a taste of such delights. There would also be lots of music at the fair and a great many pipers in attendance. At this thought he became sad, as he believed his father when he said that he would never amount to anything as a piper.

He hadn't noticed that he had walked a fair distance along the beach and was close to the mouth of a great cave in the cliffs. Just as he reached it he gave a great sigh and said, 'Och, how I wish I could be a piper.'

'Would you really like to be a piper, young Iain,' came a voice as soft and gentle as the wind.

Surprised, Iain looked up to see a little old woman, all dressed in green, with long flowing golden hair streaked with white, looking at him. She was standing between him and the cave and he suddenly thought, 'That's where she came from; she must be a fairy.' He was surprised and a bit frightened; he had been told often enough that fairies were dangerous creatures.

'Well, Iain,' she smiled, 'what is your answer? Would you like to be a piper?'

Iain nodded, unable to speak.

'Well, you must answer me a question,' said the little old woman. 'Which would you rather be, a really good piper or a rich one?'

Iain's mind started racing. If he were rich his family could get more land and more cattle and he could get a new set of pipes. But, he thought, what would be the point of playing his own pipes if he wasn't good enough to please his father.

'I would rather be a good piper than a rich one,' he said decisively.

'That is a good answer,' said the old fairy, 'now throw that old black chanter into the sea.'

'What?' he gasped, instinctively tightening his grip on the old chanter.

'You must do as I tell you,' the fairy said in a voice that clearly demanded obedience.

What if it's a trick, he thought, the fairies are always playing tricks on humans. Maybe she's just trying to take my chanter away from me. But even as he was thinking this, it was as if his arm took on a life of its own. Back it went and he threw the chanter as hard as he could. Away out over the sea it seemed to fly before falling with a splash into the water.

'Well done, Iain MacCrimmon,' the fairy said. 'Now take this chanter.'

The fairy held out a beautiful silver chanter. It was the most beautiful thing he had ever seen.

Tentatively he reached out and took the chanter, turning it over and over in his hands. It was magnificent.

'Now, Iain,' she went on, 'put it to your lips and think of a tune.'

He did so and thought of the difficult piece he had heard a couple of weeks before when a piper friend of his father's had come to visit. It was a march that was very hard to play and he remembered the piper saying it had taken him a good while to learn the piece. He put the chanter to his lips and blew. All of a sudden his fingers knew exactly what to do. He was playing the tune! And he was playing it well. This was too good to be true.

'Well done,' the fairy smiled. 'You will be a fine piper all your days now Iain, but always treat the silver chanter with respect. Do not let anyone else ever play it.' And, as swiftly as she had appeared, she was gone.

When Iain's father and brothers were on their way home from the fair that evening and about a mile from the house, they heard bagpipes. The sound was clearly coming from their home so they ran the last mile to see who had come to visit. When they came close to the house they saw a diminutive figure, dwarfed by the old set of pipes he was carrying, but playing away like a champion. They were amazed to see it was their own wee Iain.

From that day on Iain's playing went from strength to strength and word of his skill soon spread across the island. It wasn't long before he was being asked to play for weddings, and soon the chief of the MacLeods himself asked him to play up at the castle. Now the fairy had asked him if he wanted to be rich and he had said no to her, but in truth his playing was good enough to ensure that he had a pretty comfortable way of life. In the things that mattered he knew fine well that he had become rich. He met and married a beautiful young lass and in time they came to have three sons, all of whom became pipers themselves. Following in their father's footsteps they became part of the great MacCrimmon legacy, known throughout Scotland. It would be fair to say that Iain MacCrimmon had a rich and full life.

He grew older and, one after the other, his sons found wives of their own, even his youngest. By now he had a couple of grandchildren and all of his family were healthy and happy. A man could ask for little more. But then there came a fateful day when again he heard the call of the fairy. Iain had long known that this day would come.

He called his family together and told them it was time for him to go. At first they didn't understand, then his wife realised what he meant. She cried and tried to get him to stay, but Iain was adamant. Handing his old set of pipes to his eldest son, he took the silver chanter. Then, after embracing his wife, children and grandchildren, Iain MacCrimmon set off alone to the cave on the beach where all those years before he had received the fairy gift. As he went he played the chanter, and his weeping family watched as he headed for the beach. He walked along the beach till he came to the cave where the fairy was waiting. Without losing a beat he followed the fairy into the cave at Harlosh. For a while the music could be heard on the still morning air but then there was silence. Since that day no one has ever seen anything of Iain MacCrimmon, but throughout all the years that have passed the cave has been known as the Piper's Cave.

In The Piper's Cave at Boreraig

It was told that some of the MacCrimmon pipers used to go to the Piper's Cave on the beach near Boreraig, on Skye. It was somewhere they could practice without being overheard by anyone. This would let them learn new pieces without the embarrassment of being known to have to practise, or even worse, of being heard playing wrong notes! So it was a handy place. It was the habit of some of them to go down to the cave and stay there without food till they had mastered a new tune they were composing. Nowadays we tend to think of the pibrochs they composed as being primarily laments. This wasn't the case, though the coronachs, or laments, have long been a great part of the piping repertoire. Down in the cave they composed marches, battle tunes, warning tunes, praise songs and salutes – and even satires. The range was remarkable and the cave saw the composition of many masterpieces.

One time, however, one of the MacCrimmons was having real problems. He wanted a new tune for a forthcoming competition, to be attended by pipers from all over Scotland, and really wanted something special to unveil on the day. He went to the cave several times to try and compose a new tune but was getting nowhere.

Then, late one evening as he sat disconsolate in the cave, he heard the sound of a bagpipe starting. He looked up and there before him was a piper, not unlike himself but playing a very old-fashioned set of pipes. He began to march up and down the cave playing a beautiful sweet tune, and as he marched MacCrimmon realised that this was a spirit. It was one of his ancestors, come to help him in his hour of need. The piper sat spellbound as the spirit piper played the tune through once. Then, before MacCrimmon could say or do anything, the apparition vanished. Immediately he grabbed his own pipes and tried to play the melody he had just heard. He got some of it but not anywhere near all of the tune. By now it was late in the night. He resolved to go home and come again to the cave the next night, when he would try to remember the tune.

The following night he got no further than he had the night before. He had the first part of the tune but could remember no more. He had just put down his pipes to have a drink of water when again he heard the spirit bagpipes start. He turned and there was his ancestor once more, marching up and down the cave. He listened as intently as he could and once again, after one playing, the spirit vanished. He was sure he had it and started playing. Yes, he thought, I have it now, as he continued past what he had learned the night before. But again he was frustrated; he couldn't remember how the tune finished. It was a grand tune, how could he not remember the rest of it. Still, the spirit had come to him twice; perhaps it might come a third time.

The following night he returned to the cave, hoping that the spirit would come again. It was a fine tune and he knew it could easily win him the coming competition. This time he sat and waited and, sure enough, again late in the night, the spirit came. Once more he listened intently as the spirit played the tune, the sound reverberating through the cave. Then as suddenly as it had appeared, again the spirit disappeared. But this time as it began to fade, the wraith looked straight at MacCrimmon and smiled.

His heart almost bursting with excitement, he picked up his pipes and launched into the tune. He played it all the way through. He had it! He was delighted and played the tune time and again till the morning light began to streak the sky, when at last he went off home to sleep.

A few weeks later the competition came round. As ever, people were expecting great things of MacCrimmon, and no one was disappointed. He played the new tune he had learned and was the clear winner, playing what he called 'MacCrimmon's Sweetheart'.

The End of the MacCrimmons

After the 1745 rebellion it took a while for the Highlands to settle down. For a few years several of the Jacobites continued to live like guerrillas, lifting cattle to survive and constantly dodging government patrols. However, by the mid-1750s the Highlands were becoming peaceful again, though by now the clearances were beginning. People whose forefathers had lived in the same spot for untold generations were driven off to live in the growing Scottish and English cities or forced to emigrate. However, the government had not finished with the Highlanders. Long before the '45 itself, the Black Watch had been formed and the Highland soldiers were so successful that other Highland regiments were formed. Still, not all young men in the Highlands considered a life in the British army to be a good one and there were times when recruiting was very slow indeed.

It was at times like these that the government resorted to press gangs. For many years the British navy kept up its numbers by the blatant kidnapping of citizens and the army too was not above such behaviour. After all, the men pressed into service had no money, did not have the right to vote, and were, from the point of view of the officer class, expendable.

There were always those who were willing to help the government. And among them was MacLeod of Dunvegan, whose attempt to sell some of his own people into slavery in the American plantations showed his concern for his clansmen. So, when the government asked him to help 'recruit' men, he did not hesitate. It seems likely he would have asked how much he was to be paid before agreeing. At this time the MacCrimmons were still providing the pipers to Clan MacLeod; the current incumbent, Iain Mor, Big John, was a large powerful man, known for his prodigious strength. So MacLeod thought, 'Who better to lead the press gang than the piper himself?' The gang was organised and targets selected – after all they were dealing with fellow clansmen on Skye and had a fair idea of which young men they could kidnap and turn over to the government. Nowadays we see this for what it was, a form of government-sanctioned slavery, but times were harder then. Anyway, the party set off with MacCrimmon in charge to round up a bunch of healthy young men.

They decided to start their sweep in Durinish to the west of Dunvegan Castle. One of the lads they had targeted was an only son, and his mother was a widow, but this mattered little to MacLeod. MacCrimmon came with his men to fetch him. The lad spotted them from inside the house, a standard tigh dubh with double stone walls filled with heather and thatched with the same material. The poverty of the people at the time meant also that it did not have glass panes in the windows, just piles of heather to keep out the wind and cold. So the young lad simply threw the heather out of one of the back windows, climbed out, replaced the heather and made off for the hills. He intended hiding out at MacLeod's Tables. These are two striking flat-topped hills west of Dunvegan and had got their name because of a bet between the MacLeod chief and James VII in the late years of the seventeenth century.

MacLeod had been a guest at the king's palace of Holyrood in Edinburgh. One evening, dining in the great hall, James had turned to his guest and said, 'I doubt that back in Skye you have so large and magnificent a table or such remarkable candle sconces as you see here tonight, MacLeod.'

'Well, your majesty, I beg to differ,' replied the chief.

'What on earth do you mean?' asked the king, intrigued at the reply.

'Well, sire, if you will do me the courtesy of being my guest at Dunvegan Castle, I can show you a much grander table, and even more remarkable candle sconces,' he said with a smile. Now the king was sure that there was no place in the whole of Scotland that was as magnificent as Holyrood, so he decided there and then to test MacLeod's word.

It was only a few months later when the king, with a large retinue of courtiers and soldiers, arrived on Skye. He came from his ship at Dunvegan to be met by MacLeod just as the sun was setting.

'Well, MacLeod,' demanded the king as he reached the castle gates, 'where is this great dining table you say you have?'

'If you will just follow me, sire,' said the MacLeod, leading his king away from the castle to where a group of horses was tethered. They mounted and rode off into the night till they came to the foot of a hill, not that far off.

Here they dismounted and MacLeod led James and his courtiers up the side of a hill. Just as they reached the top MacLeod asked the king to walk beside him. They crested the hill, and there before them was a flat hilltop with upwards of three hundred MacLeods, each holding a flaming torch. On the sward in front of the newly, arrived party was a great feast.

'There you are, my lord,' said MacLeod. 'This is a much grander dining table than yours in Holyrood and I think you will agree that my candle sconces are easily the match of yours.'

Delighted at the conceit, the king burst into laughter and the company tucked into the arranged feast. The hilltop, and its companion beside it, were thereafter known as MacLeod's Tables.

It was here that the widow's son decided to hide out. From the top he would be able to see anyone looking for him, and he thought that he could make his escape if things looked too dangerous to stay. However, the men chasing him were also locals with a great knowledge of the area and it didn't take long for them to find and capture him. He was taken back to Dunvegan Castle and put in the dungeon with several other young fellows, ready to be transported away into the army.

The day after the boy's capture, MacLeod was told he had a visitor at the castle gate. He went down to see who it was. There stood the widow, who like her parents and their parents before them was herself a MacLeod.

'What is it?' demanded the chief.

'You are the descendant of Great Torquil of the Eagles, father and benefactor of the MacLeods,' she said, looking him straight in the eye.

'Aye, that I am,' he replied, wondering what she was going on about.

'Well, MacLeod, your men came and raided my home like wild caterans among their own people and drove away my son. I have but the one son; he is my entire family. He ran to the hills, where he was captured by your men, led by John MacCrimmon,' she said in a clear strong voice.

'Yes,' he replied again. 'And what of it?'

'Well, MacLeod,' the woman said, drawing herself up to her full height and seeming years younger, 'I have come to ask that you send my son back with me his mother. He is my sole support and as our chief you should not be treating us like this.'

'Ach, away with you woman,' he shouted. 'The government needs men to defend our country and who are you to think you can go against that?'

'You will not return my son to me?' the woman asked in a quieter tone of voice.

'No, I will not. Now be gone before I set the dogs on you,' sneered the laird.

'Well,' she said, 'it was not you who laid hands on my son, but by the powers that we all know, I tell you this: few will be the days and small will be the end of the MacCrimmons you used to do your dirty work for you.' At that she turned and marched away, stiff-backed and holding her head high.

And from that day on John MacCrimmon found himself unable to play in public. He could only find the breath to blow his pipes if he sat in a darkened room. So MacLeod had to have his piper playing in a dark room away from any company he might have, a situation that infuriated the haughty laird. And, within a generation, the piping MacCrimmons were no more and a long line of great pipers was at an end. The curse of the widow came to pass because of MacLeod's disdain for his own clansmen, and the result was the end of the MacCrimmons.

Music to Soothe the Savage Beast, Or Not

One of Scotland's longest glens is Glenlyon in Perthshire. It is a glen steeped in history, with many a remnant of ancient habitations scattered along its twenty-odd miles, from the slopes of Beinn Mhonach to the Appin of Dull. Now, a long time ago there used to be a fine family of pipers called McGregor living in Glenlyon. It is said that one of them had been taught by the MacCrimmons and was in fact the favourite pupil of the leading MacCrimmon of his day. In fact, so fond was master of pupil that he came down to Perthshire from Skye to visit him at the head of Glenlyon, not far from the edge of the great moor of Rannoch. Of course it was just a matter of a few minutes before it was suggested the great man 'had a blaw' on the pipes. This was a fair time ago, and although three drone pipes were in existence they were still not that common. A two-drone set of pipes was to hand and MacCrimmon began to play just outside McGregor's croft.

Rarely had the locals heard anything quite so good. The roof of the byre shook and the rafters shivered with the power of his playing. Attracted by the sound, a neighbour came to the croft carrying a new set of three-drone pipes, which he offered to MacCrimmon to play. This was not the first three-drone set MacCrimmon had seen. In fact he had a set back on Skye and he was well aware of the greater power of the new pipes.

'Are all the beasts in the byre securely tied?' asked the piper. On being assured they were, he blew into the pipes and launched into a virtuoso march that could be heard for miles. The man blew for a good hour, and when he finished some of the crowd went into the byre. They found that the cattle had worked their bindings loose and were covered with the perspiration of terror. Music may soothe the savage breast but MacCrimmon's piping surely terrified the beasts that day at Rannoch.

Competitions

There is a tradition of piping competitions that seems to be very old indeed. Apart from organised competitions at both local and national levels there are also stories where the competition is much more personal, so personal in the case of MacRaing that it led to his killing his rival. In other stories, as in that of the 'Glas Mheur', we see another, gentler side of humanity, with a practical lesson in how to handle the cold weather thrown in.

A Piping Challenge

Now, the MacCrimmons weren't the only men who were hereditary pipers amongst the Scottish clans. There were Mackays, who piped for the Mackenzies of Gairloch; the MacLeans of Coll had the Rankins and the Menzies had the MacIntyres as hereditary pipers. In most clans, of course, the pipers were normally members of the clan, and thus relations of the chief. Another clan that had pipers from outside were the MacDonalds, the descendants of the original Lords of the Isles who had ruled over the Hebrides and much of Scotland's west coast. Their pipers were of the MacArthur clan, a clan which up till the fifteenth century was the most influential of all the clans in Argyle. Now, Sir Alexander MacDonald came to visit MacLeod at Dunvegan in the time of Patrick Og MacCrimmon and he was mightily impressed by the piper.

'I would like to send over a young piper to study with Patrick Og,' MacDonald said to McLeod, who agreed to the idea right away.

'The thing is,' went on MacDonald, 'I would like Patrick to keep him here till he thinks McArthur is as good as his master, before he sends him home. Would that be all right?' MacLeod looked at MacCrimmon, who nodded, so he said, 'That's fine, send the lad whenever you are ready.' And the two chiefs shook hands on the deal.

Shortly after this, MacDonald went back to his own home at Finlaggan and, after another little while, Charles MacArthur arrived at Dunvegan to begin his learning under Patrick Og MacCrimmon.

From the very first they got on well. Patrick was not that much older than Charles, whom he found to be a fine musician and a ready pupil. In fact they got on so well that it was all of eleven years before Charles eventually got back to MacDonald's castle, by which time of course he was a grand piper. As a courtesy to the MacDonald, McLeod asked Patrick Og if he would take MacArthur back home and he was happy to do this. When they arrived, MacDonald had a visitor, Iain Dall. Blind Ian was a Mackay and was reckoned to be the very finest piper in the Gairloch; his reputation almost matched that of Patrick Og. MacDonald was there to greet the two pipers as they stepped ashore from the boat they had come in and he told them right off to follow him, but to remain silent. Puzzled, the two pipers followed the chief into the castle and into the great hall. There sat Iain Dall Mackay and the pipers at once realised what was to happen.

'Now, Iain Dall, I have a wee test for you,' the chief said. 'I have just had Charles MacArthur come back to me after many years studying with Patrick Og MacCrimmon and I would like you to give me your opinion on his playing.'

'Och, I will be happy to do that,' said the blind piper, standing up and waiting to be introduced to the younger piper. But the chief said nothing and neither did MacArthur. Iain Dall was aware that there was a third man in the room, but no one introduced them. Then, at a signal from the MacDonald, Charles began to play. It was immediately obvious that this was a master piper and he played on for a good ten minutes before being signalled to stop.

'Now then, Iain. What do you think of Charles as a piper?' the chief asked the blind man.

'Och, he is very good, very good indeed. I think he will have no problems at all; he will do well. You can be sure of that,' Mackay replied.

'Well then, Iain, your work isn't over. I decided I should have a choice so I sent another piper over with him to learn from Patrick. Would you like to give me your opinion of him, too?' MacDonald said, smiling.

'Well, I will tell you that if he can match your MacArthur man here, he will be a very fine piper indeed,' came the reply.

At that Patrick Og struck up a tune and marched up and down the hall. From almost the moment the second piper began, Iain Dall began to smile. He sat there as Patrick Og played, with his legs crossed and his arms folded, listening intently.

When Patrick finished, MacDonald asked Iain Dall what he thought.

'Well, there's no need to try me in that matter. I know fine well who that was playing. I need no vision for I have not lost the eyes of my understanding. I would know him amongst a thousand pipers. It is my old friend Patrick Og MacCrimmon.'

The other two pipers and the chief burst out laughing and, as MacCrimmon introduced MacArthur to the blind piper, the chief called for a drink for the pipers. He was proud to have three such great musicians in his house and, after Iain Dall had played as well, they all four sat down and celebrated their meeting. The pipes kept being played and the bottle being passed till sun streaked the sky the following morning. It was a fine homecoming for Charles MacArthur and he and the other two pipers were lifelong friends after that.

A Piper's Revenge

For thousands of years there has been contact between Scotland and Ireland. Rathlin Island off the Ulster coast was officially a part of the Hebrides until the eighteenth century and people have been going back and forth over the Sheuch, as the North Channel of the Irish Sea is commonly known, since time immemorial. One Irishman who came over to the island of Mull was Cu-Duilg MacRaing and he is said to have been the very first piper on the island. He became attached to the clan MacLean on Mull and, like some other fortunate pipers, it seems the fairies liked him and gave him a few tunes, including 'The Finger Lock'. Though, as we shall see, he got the tune in rather a roundabout fashion. He was also said to have been given the remarkable gift of a fairy chanter. He was a good piper and like many another before him he became totally absorbed into the clan MacLean. However, he was a man who had a bit of a temper and his judgement wasn't always quite what it should be.

Years after he had come over from Ireland, a couple of other Irishmen came to Mull: a harpist and a blacksmith. Now the blacksmith, whose name was Robert, wanted his son Callum to learn to play the pipes. Callum had a good ear but was an idle sort of fellow and didn't practice nearly as hard as MacRaing thought he should. This infuriated the piper, as he saw it as a sign of disrespect to himself. One night Callum accompanied MacRaing to a wedding where they were to play, and the young lad disgraced himself by drinking too much whisky. People had kept offering him the drink and he thought it disrespectful to refuse, so he drank all that was offered and, being young yet, couldn't really handle it too well. In fact he fell over. MacRaing, furious at this insensitivity, and already tired of the lad's lack of application, threw him out of the house. In truth, MacRaing's pride was hurt and this was something he just could not stomach. So the young lad found himself out on the moor at midnight, in unfamiliar parts. Despite his condition, he spotted a light about a mile away and headed for it. He fell on several occasions but felt no pain, and just carried on towards the light. At last he came to an old black house and went straight in.

There, sitting at the fire, was an old, old man, who welcomed him in to sit and warm himself by the fire. The old man proceeded to tell Callum that, as they spoke, MacRaing was composing a new tune and only lacked one variation to have it finished.

The old man then said, 'I will teach you the tune here and now and, once you have learned it, I want you to go and play it for MacRaing.'

The old man was clearly a fairy – he could be nothing else – but Callum was fired up with the whisky and felt no fear whatsoever. So the fairy proceeded to teach the apprentice piper the variation of the tune, and, once he was satisfied with the lad's playing of it, he told him, 'Now go to where MacRaing is and let him hear it. Just you walk up and down outside his window, playing the tune, and he'll catch on.'

So Callum headed back to the house where he had earlier disgraced himself. MacRaing was sitting, mulling over the new composition in his room, when he heard pipes start to blow outside his window. He listened and almost immediately knew that this was the last variation he needed for the tune he had been working on. He ran to the window and was taken aback at the sight of Callum, his wastrel of a pupil, marching up and down playing this marvellous tune.

Once he heard how Callum had got the tune, however, he realised he was being blessed by the fairies and his attitude to the young lad softened considerably. He took the lad back on and continued to teach him, and in time Callum became a fine piper. It wasn't long after this that Callum and his father, the blacksmith, went back to Ireland. MacRaing understood how fortunate he had been to have been given the tune by the fairies, but, not being the most generous of souls, he wanted no one else on Mull to hear it. He wanted to keep the tune for himself and for his own pleasure alone. Every so often he would go off to a cave hidden behind the waterfall known as the Eas Fors, to play the hidden tune, which eventually became known as 'The Finger Lock'.

Unusually, MacRaing's daughter wanted to learn the pipes. In those days, if women were musically talented they tended to concentrate on the clarsach (harp). However, MacRaing was intrigued by his daughter's interest and he decided to humour her. Because she was family he had no reluctance in teaching her his 'hidden tune', though she had to accompany him to the cave behind the waterfall to be taught it. And she was only allowed to play it there behind the curtain of water, in case anyone else heard the tune and learned it. A few years later, when the first flush of womanhood was on her, a young man came to be taught to play the pipes. Unknown to her father she took a fancy to the young lad, and he responded. So it came about that, totally unknown to her father, she taught the stranger 'The Finger Lock'. It was only as the young man was leaving that the situation became clear. MacRaing asked him to play all the tunes he had learned and when the laddie stopped he encouraged him to play some more. At this point the hapless lad began to play 'The Finger Lock', and MacRaing reached for his sword. Tradition is silent as to whether the young piper escaped or was cut down on the spot by his tutor, but we can be pretty sure that his daughter never made the same mistake again! This episode is, however, illustrative of MacRaing's temper.

One time a couple of pipers came all the way from to Northumberland from Mull. In those far-off days the bagpipes were still relatively popular south of the border. One of the Northumbrian pipers, hearing of MacRaing's reputation, decided to come over to Kilbrennan to challenge the Irishman to a piping competition. The challenge was of course accepted, and they both chose locations in which to play their pieces. The Northumberland piper gave his renditions from Dun Chagain, thought to be an old Norse fort above Kilbrennan, while MacRaing played in his usual position on a knoll behind his home, which was given the name 'Cnoc nam Piobairean', the hill of the pipers. MacRaing was adjudged to be the winner, but when the Englishman came back the following year and challenged him again, this time the Irishman was beaten. For a third year running the Northumberland piper came back to Mull and again he challenged the Irish piper. MacRaing won again, but he realised how close it had been; he had barely beaten the Englishman and wasn't sure he could do so again if he came back again the following year. The Englishman was improving steadily and MacRaing felt certain that in another year the man would be a better piper than him. This preyed on his mind till he convinced himself it would be an affront to his pride to let the situation develop any further.

When the Northumberland piper left to return home, the Irishman sneaked off, unnoticed by anyone, and followed him, keeping out of sight. He caught up with him at Achadashenaig on the other side of the river from Aros Castle. Coming up to the Englishman, he drew his sword and cried, 'Defend yourself.' Although the Northumberland piper was armed and could use his sword if necessary, he was no match for MacRaing. In the ensuing fight MacRaing killed the poor Englishman and buried him just where he fell. The spot became known thereafter as 'Dail an-t-Sassunnaich', the Field of the Englishman. It was one way to prevent competition.

There was another Irishman who was a regular autumn visitor to Mull. He was a nobleman of sorts and one year he decided to bring his piper over from Ireland with him. The Irish pipes had, of course, to meet up with MacRaing, the best piper on the island

and a fellow Irishman. So one night they sat in a room in Duart Castle, just the two of them, and played together. Whatever MacRaing played, the Irishman matched him. When MacRaing finished one particular set of tunes the Irishman played the same set, note for note, but reversed the position of his hands to right hand up and left hand down. This was extremely difficult and MacRaing took it as a personal challenge. He had to match the Irishman, so he too began to play 'upside down'. He managed up to a point. He had a problem with the little finger of his right hand. Try as he might he just could not get it right. Mortified, and driven by his fierce pride, his anger overwhelmed him and he whipped out his dirk, cut off the offending finger and stomped off to get some whisky.

Later that night the two visiting Irishmen were catching up on what they had been doing that day. 'Well,' said the piper, 'I was playing tunes with the MacRaing fellow, and something really strange happened.'

'What was that?' asked the nobleman.

'Well, you know the trick I do when I reverse my hands and carry on playing?'

'Surely I do,' replied the other.

'That really got to MacRaing, and he had to try it too,' he continued.

'And how did he manage it?' asked his companion.

'Up to a point, you know, he was pretty good,' the piper told him. 'But he couldn't get his little finger on the right hand to do as he wanted. Now, I've met many a man with a bit of pride, but this one is something altogether different. When his little finger wouldn't do what he wanted, sure, didn't he out with his little knife and cut the damned thing off! The man is definitely not all there.'

The Irish nobleman realised that this incredible situation had put him and his piper into grave danger. When MacLean heard of what MacRaing had done he would undoubtedly blame it on the visiting Irishmen – it was unlikely that the clan chief would put it down to MacRaing's mad temper. They would be lucky to escape with their lives. So at dead of night they left the castle and headed to Tobermory to try to find a boat to take them back to Ireland.

In the morning when MacLean arose, he asked after his guests, only to be told that they had disappeared in the night. MacLean immediately thought that they must have been up to something underhand, to sneak off like thieves in the night, so he decided to go after them to Tobermory. Just as he was ready to set off he heard the story of what MacRaing had done and, as the Irish nobleman had predicted, decided it was the fault of the Irishmen rather than MacRaing. He wanted revenge. The fact that MacRaing had cut off his own finger did not seem to be of any consequence to MacLean; he felt he had been insulted and in his own home too. By the time he got to Tobermory with half a dozen of his men, he found the Irishmen had already crossed over to Ardnamurchan. So he too crossed over to the mainland and eventually caught up with them at Kilchoan. There he killed and buried them both before returning home. On hearing the news, MacRaing composed a sad and beautiful coronach for the two Irishmen, 'The Lament for the Lord of the Meeting', which was rumoured to have been played in Canada in the early twentieth century but is known no more in Scotland.

The Glas Mheur Pibroch

A long time ago on the Ardnish peninsula, opposite the isle of Eigg, there was a great gathering of pipers in the days coming up to Hogmanay. As it was a time of national celebration it had seemed a good idea to have a competition. It was a hard winter all across Scotland and the day itself was freezing cold. However, in those days no Highlander worth his salt would be seen wearing gloves. It was so viciously cold that no one could finger their chanter properly for more than a minute and even with liberal doses of whisky the whole day seemed to be destined to be a bit of an anti-climax. Despite the time of year, it had been decided that the competition should be held outside, so great fires were lit to try and warm things up. But still all the pipers' fingers felt like ice. They were blowing on their fingers, rubbing their hands together and keeping their hands in the warm folds of their plaids, but within a minute or so after starting to play they all felt their fingers grow numb, making proper and clear fingering virtually impossible.

There was one piper who was a bit late for the gathering; as he was hurrying along to the gathering site he met a dairymaid on the road. She was a big, strong, handsome woman, who seemed to be in her early twenties, and despite the cold her arms were bare, as were her feet and her fine big neck had no scarf or shawl around it. Sure, her skin looked a little red but she was a glowing picture of health. They greeted each other and the piper said, 'I reckon it's too cold to play well on a day like this.'

'There's plenty before you on the road saying the same thing,' she replied with a smile.

They stood and chatted about nothing much at all and after a bit he said, 'Would you look at my hands. They're in no fit state for playing the pipes this day – I'll never manage a note at all.'

At that the lassie's smile grew bigger and she said, 'Well, if you like I can maybe help you, but you must do as I say. All right?' As she said it her eyes twinkled.

'Well,' he says, a little suspicious, 'as long as it's right and proper,' and maybe he had a wee glint in his eye as well, despite the weather.

'Och, behave yourself,' she said and blushed. 'I wouldn't ask you to do anything that wasn't right and proper; we've only just met. Come with me.'

And she led him through the frozen grass to an old well just a few yards off the road, which you wouldn't know was there, hidden as it was in the grass and scrub. All around the well there were icicles and, breaking some off, she rubbed her hands with them as if they were slivers of soap.

'You do the same now,' she told him.

A bit reluctantly, and thinking his hands were cold enough already, but remembering he had promised to do what he was told, he broke off some of the icicles and rubbed them all over his hands. In little more than a minute his hands began to tingle. Soon they were really warm and his fingers were supple and strong.

'Thank you, thank you, that's just wonderful,' he said.

'Och, they'll be warm for a few hours yet – off you go and play, but let me know on the way back how you got on. I'll be just up there,' and she pointed to a wee house about half a mile away on the side of a hill overlooking the road.

So off he goes and, of course, none of the others could play more than a note or two, while he marched up and down blowing and playing for nearly an hour and they all had to admit that, on the day, he was the champion. He did drop in to see the dairy-maid on his way home and his hands were still as warm as when they met. Maybe she found that out for herself, for she was a handsome lass and the piper was young himself. The tune he played was known ever after as the 'Pibroch Glas Mheur' – meaning the locked fingers, because none of the other pipers could play at all. But I think it might better be called 'the helpful lass by the road'.

Pipers and the Supernatural

⊰◈⊱

The motif of the fairy gift that we have seen in some of the MacCrimmon stories is a widespread one. The fairies, however, are devious creatures and, as is shown in several of the following tales, their gifts have to be treated with respect and, usually, secrecy. While the heroes of some of the following tales fall prey to the power of fairies, witches and other supernatural creatures, there are also instances where pipers, through their courage, have managed to escape from that power, in one case even thwarting the Queen of the Fairies herself. The motif of the musicians being lured into fairy hills for a night, only to discover afterwards they have been absent for a hundred years or more, is a relatively common one and there are many instances of similar tales concerning fiddlers. These stories are perhaps a faint echo of ancient memories of rituals that used to happen at fairy mounds (also called knowes). Often these mounds turn out to have been ancient tumuli, or burial mounds. It has been suggested that these chambered cairns and other tumuli were the sites of rituals where people tried to contact their ancestors to ask for their help in such significant matters as ensuring that the crops would grow in the coming seasons. The most important of these rituals probably took place on the Night of the Dead, what we today call Hallowe'en, which was believed to be the time when the barriers between the land of the living and the dead were at their weakest. The fact that so many of these burial chambers held the remains of considerable numbers of people, usually just their skull and thigh bones, shows that they were certainly used communally.

Uamha an Oir, the Cave of Gold

Long ago on Skye people were terrified by a monster that lived in the Cave of Gold, called Uamha an Oir, on the beach near Kilmuir. It was said that deep within the cave there was a large pot of gold and the monster guarded it. The problem was that the creature had taken to raiding the neighbouring villages and clachans and taking away cattle and sometimes even humans to feed its ravenous appetite. However, it was such a gruesome beast that no one was prepared to tackle it, and the few who had tried were all killed. Now, at the time there was a famous piper living nearby, a MacArthur, one of the hereditary pipers to the MacDonald Lords of the Isles. Thus he was a man of some standing in the community and he felt that it was his duty to try and get rid of this dreadful beast.

MacArthur was a fine warrior even though he wasn't particularly big and strong. He knew that it wouldn't be easy to take on the beast and that his struggle would be long and hard, with no guarantee that he himself would return, even if he managed to slay the foul creature. Despite all these problems he swore an oath that he would kill the beast or die in the trying. His family were distraught; the thing in the cave had killed many warriors in the past and they were certain they were going to lose the head of their family.

Before setting out on the fateful day, MacArthur played a new tune on his pipes. He had also written words to it, words that show he had accepted the doom he had chosen for himself and was bravely set on fulfilling the oath he had made to rid Kilmuir of this foul monster. These are the words that have come down to us:

I shall come never, never return
Ere I return from the Cave of Gold

The kidling flocks will be goats on the rocks
And the children will be warriors bold
I am woe, woe, under spells to go
I'll be for aye in the Cave of Gold.

Clearly he knew that he had little chance of survival. Anyway, off he went to the cave, his pipes skirling with a fiery march. Without hesitation he went straight in and those of his family and friends who had followed at a distance, their hearts full of foreboding, heard the pipes for quite a few minutes. Then the tune of the pipes changed and stopped. Immediately the waiting people heard these ominous words:

Pity me, without hands three
Two for the pipes and a sword hand free.

This was followed by a horrible noise, a roaring and yelling, with occasional sounds of the pipes, then silence. No one dared go into the cave. They waited all that day and through the night but there was no sign of MacArthur. And nor has there been a sign of him since, but from that day on the people of Kilmuir were free of the monster. It was never seen again and the people realised that, though MacArthur had died in his quest to free the area of the foul beast, the quest had succeeded and he had killed the monster in the Cave of Gold.

A Long Night's Playing

One day not too long ago a couple of strange and wild-looking characters were seen in the streets of Inverness. Both were dressed in the breacan, or plaid, the original and true Highland dress that is aped by the modern kilt. They were heading towards the town centre from the direction of Tomnahurich – the hill of the yew trees. Long a burial ground and associated for even longer with the fairies, Tomnahurich is just south of the centre of Inverness and overlooks the river. Some say the Queen of the Fairies holds court there and others that Finn MacCoul, the great Gaelic warrior hero, sleeps within the hill with his warriors, awaiting the day when they have to ride forth to save the country. At first people merely gave quizzical looks to the two Highlanders, though some people noticed that the Gaelic they were speaking to each other was a little strange. It wasn't till they had come close to the centre of the town and started shouting and kicking at cars that the police were called.

It took half a dozen brawny Inverness policemen to take them into custody, for they were clearly angry and upset. However, none of the policemen could get much sense out of them, so they were assumed to be drunk and were thrown into a cell till the morning. Come the morning they were brought up before the sheriff, who asked them what they thought they were up to. They just looked at him and at each other with clenched brows and gritted teeth. One of the clerks of the court approached the sheriff and whispered in his ear. He repeated his question to the two men, but this time in Gaelic.

As soon as the sheriff started speaking in Gaelic both of the men started speaking at once, rushing to tell their story.

'Wheesht,' said the sheriff, 'just one at a time. You,' he said, pointing to the man on the left of the dock, 'you tell me what happened.'

The tale the man told was truly amazing.

'We were on our way, sir, from Strathspey to play in the streets in Inverness when this old man stopped us on the road. He had seen our pipes and asked us if we would like to play for a dance. He said he would pay us a guinea each and as much uisge beatha (whisky) as we could drink. This was a fair offer, we thought, so we decided to play for the man. He took us inside Tomnahurich, honestly, sir, through a big door we hadn't seen before and there was a great crowd of ladies and gentlemen ready for a dance. The whole place, a great big hall it was, was lit by candles and they gave us a drink to start us off. We played through the night, sir, and come the morning the man gave us our pay and we came down to the town. But everything has changed, hasn't it, Donald?' he asked, turning to his friend in the dock beside him.

'Ochone, Ochone, I do not recognise the place at all hardly now,' said his companion, with a frightened look in his eye.

'You say this was just last night you played for the old man?' inquired the sheriff.

'Aye, sir, it was just last night.'

'And did you get paid alright?' the sheriff continued.

'Aye, we did,' replied Donald. 'A golden guinea each.'

The sheriff turned to the court to speak to the police sergeant sitting there.

'Did you find any money on these men when you searched them?' he demanded.

'No, sir,' replied the sergeant, standing up and then immediately sitting down.

'Excuse me, sir,' said the first piper, 'We weren't sure who these men were so we hid the money.'

'Well, hand it over now,' ordered the sheriff.

The two Highlanders ducked briefly down into the dock before standing up again, each with a bright shining guinea in his right hand.

'Hand them over to that man there,' said the sheriff, as the Clerk of the Court approached the dock. 'And you, bring them to me.'

The two pipers did as they were told and handed the guineas over. But just as they left their hands they turned to dust and the Clerk of the Court was left with a palmful of nothing but fine dust, which started to blow into the air, even though the court was perfectly still and without a draught.

'There's something funny going on here,' said the sheriff. 'We need to find out what is happening. You are remanded in custody for further enquiries. Take them down.'

Two policemen came forward and took the pipers away, with another half-dozen uniformed men in close attendance, just in case. The two pipers were led away, looking even more confused than before. They clearly had no idea what was happening to them.

Once they were in their cell they talked rapidly to each other for a few minutes and then one of them came to the cell door and called to the policeman on duty. Luckily, he was a local man and spoke Gaelic.

'Could you fetch us a priest?' Donald asked him. 'We would very much like to see a priest.'

His fearful eyes and strange manner touched the constable's heart and he went to get permission for a priest to be called.

An hour or so later, a Gaelic-speaking Catholic priest arrived at the courthouse. He had been told there was something odd going on at the courthouse, but had been given few details. He was taken aback to be met in a police cell by two Highlanders dressed in traditional style, whose clothes appeared to be ancient indeed. They were so pleased to see him that both started speaking at once. They told him they had been at the battle of Sheriffmuir just a week before heading up to Inverness and they had no idea what had happened to them. Were they in heaven, or were they in hell or where were they?

The priest was perplexed; two hundred Sheriffmuir had been fought in 1715, more than years earlier. He decided they must be mad, but what kind of madness could affect two people in exactly the same way? He was at a loss as to what to do. So he got the two Highlanders to kneel with him, and began to pray.

At the very moment he invoked the name of the Lord, something strange happened. The two men in plaids kneeling before him began to fade, and the two pipers turned to dust before his eyes. The fine dust swirled into the empty air and within a minute there was no sign that the pipers had ever existed.

Another Tomnahurich Tale

For many ages the Queen of the Fairies made her home in Tomnahurich and she ruled over her subjects with an iron will. What she wanted she would have, and such were her magic powers that no fairy ever thought to question her. From the fairy realm inside Tomnahurich she could spy on humans over a vast distance. One day she happened to notice Angus Mor, a young piper who had come to Inverness from Wester Ross to make a name for himself. Now Angus was a fine piper indeed, and he was also tall and handsome and a very fine dancer. He turned the heads of young, and not so young, women wherever he went. He was also known to be honest and open-hearted, friendly and helpful to all. The Queen of the Fairies took a shine to him and sent two of her guards out into the human world to bring him to her.

Angus was sitting outside his own door on the outskirts of Inverness when two well-dressed gentlemen came up to him.

'Are you Angus Mor, the piper?' one of them asked.

'Aye, that I am,' replied Angus, eyeing the two strangers. Whoever they were, they were not poor. Their clothes were of fine workmanship and their shoes looked very expensive indeed.

'Well we have heard that you are a grand piper indeed,' the second man said.

'It's very kind of you to say so,' Angus said. 'What can I do for you?'

'Well,' said the first one, 'our mistress is a great lady; she is holding a dance nearby tonight and she would like you to come and play for her. If you are happy to do so, we will come and pick you up at eight o'clock tonight. She said you can have double your normal fee.'

Now Angus wasn't a greedy man, but double wages were not something to be ignored, so he agreed that the two men could come and collect him later that night. It wasn't till they had gone that he realised they had given him neither their mistress's name nor the place he was to be playing. Never mind, he thought, this should be good night's work. At precisely at eight o'clock the two strangers arrived to take Angus to the ball. Off they went and pretty soon Angus realised they were heading for Tomnahurich. Like everyone else in the Highlands, he knew the reputation of the place and realised that his companions were not human. He figured out they must want him to play for the fairies to dance, but he was a courageous man and was curious to see what the fairy ball would be like. When they got to the fairy hill and he saw the great door begin to swing open his curiosity was sparked even further. He also realised that if he turned to run there was no knowing what the two fairies would do to him.

On they went and there, seated on her throne amongst thousands of magically-garbed fairies, was the Queen of the Fairies. Tall and beautiful, she was unlike anything he had ever seen.

'Welcome, Angus Mor,' she said, beckoning him to come and sit beside her, 'welcome and welcome again. You are thrice welcome.'

Angus was overwhelmed by the power and beauty of this fabulous creature and sat in the throne alongside her, looking at her beautiful pale face, long neck, rippling black hair and smooth shoulders.

'Now, Angus, I must tell you that I have you brought here because I have fallen in love with you. Your good looks, your great piping and your warm heart make you a prince amongst men. I want you to stay here with me and become my consort. You shall want for nothing that the human or the fairy worlds can give you.'

Angus' jaw dropped. He couldn't believe what he was hearing. The Queen of the Fairies wanted him to be her partner! This was fantastic! But Angus was a good man at heart and knew what he must do.

'Y-your Majesty,' he stuttered, 'that cannot be. I have a wife and child already back in Inverness and I cannot abandon them.'

He saw at once that a steely glint came into the queen's eyes as she looked at him. He could feel the tension in the air. How could anyone refuse the Queen of the Fairies?

Suddenly he sprang to his feet, pulled out the sgian dubh from his stocking top and pointed it at the queen. All the fairies flinched away at the sight of the cold steel – they have never had any power over things of iron and steel and this causes them to be greatly afraid of such things. Holding the little knife close to the queen's throat, he got round behind her and moved her towards the door.

'Open the door, or your queen dies,' he roared at the top of his voice. In truth, he didn't know if he could harm the queen, but he had to get the door open somehow. Suddenly, with no move from anyone he could see, he felt fresh air on his back. The door was open! He immediately threw himself backwards through the door, waving the knife about him as he did so. He came through the door and tumbled down the side of the hill. As soon as he found his feet, he was in a defensive stance, his pipes clutched under his left arm and his right hand moving about before him waving the knife. There was no sign of the door he had just come through or of anyone, human or fairy, there on the slopes of Tomnahurich.

He had a narrow escape. But he knew that the fairies could be vindictive and ran all the way home to his family.

When he got there, no one was about. His wife and child were gone, with a pot of food still bubbling on the fire and a chair lying on its side on the floor. The Queen of the Fairies had stolen them away!

Angus felt as if his heart would break and knelt there on the floor of his wee cottage sobbing uncontrollably. How could he ever hope to get his beautiful wife and child back from the all-powerful Queen of the Fairies? Maybe he would have to give himself up and do what the fey creature wanted. As he sat there in the deepening night by the firelight, he decided that his only course of action was to go back to Tomnahurich and give himself up. He headed straight back up to Tomnahurich but, try as he might, he could not find where the door had been. He called and cried to the queen that he would come to her but there was no sound of any reply. It slowly dawned on him that in turning the queen down he had made an enemy for life. He had heard enough tales of the vindictiveness of the fairies when crossed to realise the situation. She would make him suffer all his days now, he somehow just knew it.

He sank to his knees in the grass on the side of Tomnahurich, sobbing gently. He would never see his wife or son again. They had been spirited away by the fairies on the orders of the Fairy Queen herself.

Suddenly, he felt a light touch on his shoulder. He looked up and there was a fairy woman, almost as beautiful as the queen herself, with the same green eyes and long red hair.

'Fear not, Angus,' she said in a voice like the tinkling of a mountain stream. 'Fear not. The queen is not the only one who has taken notice of you. I too have been watching you and I know that in your heart you love your wife and will never love any other. I too have fallen in love with you, Angus Mor, but I know you will never be mine. Now, will you do what I tell you, to get your wife back?'

'Oh, yes, yes. Thank you,' Angus burst out. 'I will do anything to get them back. I am even ready to give myself to your queen.'

'Oh no,' said the fairy with a wry smile, 'now you have refused her she has no interest in anything other than making you suffer. But she is not beyond all power and hope.'

'Right,' said Angus, 'tell me what to do.'

The following evening at sunset Angus Mor stood on the hillside at Tomnahurich, just where he had been told to. Then, as the sun began to set, he began to sing an old magic song the fairy woman had taught him the previous night:

> I know the cat that was in Ulva
> With its tail turned to the fire,
> I know . . .

Just as he reached the third line of the song, the great door in the side of the hill swung open and Angus's wife and son were thrust out of the fairy hall. The queen knew that if he sang any more her own power would be threatened; she had no choice but to give him back his wife and son. Angus took his wife and son home right away and gave thanks for their rescue. What the rest of the song would have been he had no idea, but it had worked. In his heart of hearts he hoped that the fairy who helped him had been clever enough to avoid detection. Having felt the wrath of the queen's spite, he feared what might befall her. He never saw her or the fairy queen again.

What eventually became of the fairy maiden who helped we cannot be sure, but given that we humans cannot begin to fathom the power of the fairies it seems likely she escaped the queen's wrath.

A Sad End

Now, all over Scotland there are stories of pipers being lured into fairy hills. If nothing else, it serves to show just how much the fairies themselves appreciated the pipes. Some of these tales, like that of Angus Mor, have happy endings while others, like that of the lads who came out of Tomnahurich, are sad ones. There is one, however, that is particularly tragic and it is the story of a piper who lived on the isle of Lewis in the 1690s. He was a young and vigorous lad and liked nothing more than to walk through the hills and along the shores near his home playing the pipes.

On many a day his only audience was the wild animals and birds, as he often walked a fair distance from human habitation. Even in those days, when there were a lot more people in the islands than there have been for the past two hundred years, there were many areas that were relatively uninhabited. And the young piper often wandered into these areas, playing as he went. Unknown to him, though, he had another audience. The fairies of the area, who were never too bothered about being close to humans, also had homes in these isolated glens and straths. They became accustomed to the young lad's playing in out-of-the-way places and began to really appreciate his music.

So, one night as he was heading back just before dark to his clachan near Fort William, he was met on the road by an old man in a strange green costume. Now, the young lad realised right off that the old fellow was a fairy, but he had heard of how the fairies had helped pipers in the past so was intrigued by what the creature wanted to say.

'Hello, piper, would you like to play for a dance tonight?' asked the fairy, his eyes twinkling.

'Well, I might be interested, and then again I might not be,' replied the piper. 'It all depends on the payment.'

'Ah well, we will give you food and drink of the very best and three golden guineas to go with them. How would that suit you?' replied the fairy.

Now the young lad knew fine well that taking drink or food from the fairies could be very dangerous indeed, but the idea of three guineas for a night's work seemed very attractive.

'That would suit me just fine,' he said. 'I'll come along with you to play for the three guineas. In advance.'

The fairy simply smiled at him, reached into his pocket and pulled out three brand new golden guineas and handed them over.

So the pair of them went off to the fairy ball, held in a great mound that the piper had walked by a hundred times obliviously. For a goodly while he was careful not to drink or eat but, as the dancing went on and on and the excitement at being among these beautiful eldritch creatures mounted he began to get thirsty. At last, he needed to slake his thirst between two reels and accepted a good glass of whisky from a beautiful fairy woman, dressed in what looked like green silk and with amazing green eyes. He tossed off the dram and started up again; the fairies once more began to dance. Several times more he took a dram, but with all the blowing he felt his wits as sharp as ever and was sure that he would get out all right.

During one lively reel he began to move about and he felt something under his feet. He looked down and saw there was something just under the earthen floor. Something hard and straight and long. Intrigued, but not losing a beat or mis-fingering a note, he began to kick at the object with his foot. After two or three kicks, the thing burst from the earth – it was an old sword. Just at that the dance finished and, stopping playing, he bent down to touch the sword. All around him the fairies were drawing back in horror; cold iron was something they always seemed to greatly fear. As he touched the old sword he came to his senses, and at the same moment a breath of fresh cold air hit him from behind, as if a door had suddenly opened. With no hesitation he turned and ran straight out of the fairy hill, realising that he had been caught up in the magic after all. The piper took a great breath of the clear mountain air and turned to look at the fairy hill. In the first pre-dawn light there was no sign on the heather that there had ever been any door there and no sign of the shining lights of just a second or two before. The sun was just beginning to lighten the mountain tops as he made his way towards home. He felt marvellous, even if he had been up playing all night, and he thought it might be the effects of the fairy whisky – it certainly had tasted fine enough. He hadn't gone more than a mile or so when he thought to play himself a wee tune. Even after a whole night's playing he wanted to play on and wasn't tired at all. So he struck up a tune and headed down the glen, his kilt swinging.

Now, early in the morning sounds can travel a fair distance. A mile or so down the same glen a bunch of men heard the pipes and decided to see who this was coming towards them. Down the glen came the young piper in the growing dawn light. Then he saw them, stretched out across the glen. Men in redcoats with muskets, and all pointed at him. He put down his pipes and raised his arms as they came towards him. One of them spoke Gaelic and asked him what he thought he was doing. He told them what had happened, but when the soldier translated this for his companions it brought forth howls of laughter.

'You are under arrest for wearing forbidden dress and playing the war-pipes,' the soldier told him, to the piper's great bemusement. Fifty years had passed since he had gone into the hill and he had no idea of the intervening Jacobite rebellions and the cold, malicious slaughter on Culloden Moor, and after. So he was taken to Stornoway jail, tried not only for breaking the law as stated in the Disarming Act of 1746, but for flaunting it by his behaviour. Notwithstanding his story of having gone into the hill in the previous century, he was found guilty and sentence was passed. The next day he was taken out and shot as a warning to others not to wear the Highland dress or to play the bagpipes.

The Piper of Windy Ha

On the Shetland island of Fetlar there was a hill called Windy Ha and on a nearby croft at Olrig there lived a handsome young lad called Peter Malcolm. He was a cheerful young man and if he did have a bit of a high opinion of himself it was one that was shared by others, not least several of the young ladies of the district. One day he was on his way back home from the moor, where he had been cutting peat, when he came across a very bonnie young lass by the side of the road. Now, Peter was fond of the fairer sex and he was sure that he knew every young lassie on the island, but he had never seen this pretty creature before. So he decided to make her acquaintance and said hello. She replied in a voice that sounded to his ear like silver bells and, looking deep into her deep green eyes, he was smitten with her charms. To him she seemed like a creature from another planet, and when she said she could grant him a wish he accepted the idea with no hesitation. She told him he could wish for one of three things. He could wish to be a preacher and he would be the finest preacher that anyone had ever heard; he could ask for gold and he would be rich beyond the dreams of his fathers; or he could wish to become a piper and such would be his skill that he would be the very best piper in all the world.

Now Peter, like the rest of the island people, went to church regularly but he had never thought much of the preacher and was sure that his way of life would be of no interest to him. Likewise, being a sensible young man, he understood that, as his grandmother had often told him, 'enough is as good as a feast'. But when she mentioned the piping a light came into his eyes. He was well aware of the role pipers played at weddings and at dances and how often they attracted the attention of young ladies. To be admired by the ladies and respected by the men was something he could wish for. There were decided advantages to becoming a well-known piper. So he said he would be happy to become a piper. Just at that moment he noticed that the young lass had a set of pipes in her hand. And what a set of pipes they were. The drones were of ebony, mounted with gold; the chanter was chased in silver; and the bag was of the softest purple velvet.

'Now, Peter, take these pipes and be sure you can play them. All I ask in payment is that you come back here in a year and a day and play for me to let me hear just how well you can do. Is that alright?'

Bemused by the quality of the pipes he had just had handed to him, and still a bit awed by this beautiful young woman, Peter remembered his manners and thanked her profusely before turning towards Castletown and home. A few hundred yards down the road he came to his senses a bit and turned to look for the lass. She was nowhere to be seen, but the pipes were real enough, so he decided to give them a try. As soon as his lips touched the mouthpiece, his fingers flew to the holes on the chanter and he was playing a merry reel as if he had been playing for years! He carried on playing all the way home. Waiting at the door of the croft were his parents and brothers and sisters, who had all come to see just who this wonderful piper was. They were astounded to see it was their Peter. By the time they let him stop, the poor lad was exhausted and collapsed into his bed.

The following day he awoke thinking he must have been dreaming, but as soon as he picked up the pipes it seemed that every tune he had ever heard, and a lot of new ones besides, were in his fingers. Over the next few days, word spread all over the island that young Peter Malcolm had become a grand piper.

Very soon he was being asked to play at all kinds of occasions: weddings and christenings, birthday parties and dances. As the word of his talent spread, people began to come from other islands to hear him play. Happily for Peter, quite a few of them were bonny young lasses; we can be sure that he was intent on taking advantage of his popularity to have a fine old time with them. However, on a great many of the nights he performed, his appreciative audiences kept him playing till the small hours of the morning, and he had little energy to do anything but sleep. In all of this time, no one ever heard him play a wrong note or miss a beat; it seemed whatever tune he was asked to play he would have no difficulty with. His fame spread to the mainland and soon pipers were coming over from Scotland to listen to this young phenomenon; none returned home unimpressed. It seemed as if he was the king of pipers himself.

So time passed and, being so busy, Peter was surprised to realise that it was time for him to fulfil his promise to the young lass who had given him the pipes. The thought of seeing her again made his pulse quicken and the breath catch in his throat. Maybe all this time she was the one for him.

So the day came – a year and a day since he first met her. He set out towards Drawick to meet the beautiful young woman. He made his way slowly and steadily along the sands, playing as he went. Never had he sounded so clear and bright and he realised that he was playing even better than ever. And suddenly there she was, in a silver dress, standing by the side of the road on the beach where they had first met. As he came closer she began to dance. He had never seen anything so graceful in all his days. Entranced by her, he continued to play as she danced along the beach. He followed, eyes fixed on the vision of beauty. So entranced was the young piper that he did not notice she was leading him towards the great cave on Peedie Sands. On she went into the cave, and Peter followed without hesitation. In they went to the cave. It is said the music played on for a long time, but of Peter Malcolm nothing was ever seen again. It was on St John's Day he went to meet the lassie on the sands. If you go to the mouth of the cave even yet on Midsummer at the hour of midnight, you will hear the far-off playing of Peter Malcolm as he continues to entertain the Queen of the Fairies.

The Piper of Eathie

To the north of Inverness there is a peninsula known as the Black Isle. It is a beautiful part of Scotland and full of ancient remnants of our distant ancestors, such as the magnificent carved symbol stones left by the Picts. And, just as in the rest of Scotland, there were fairies. Here, at a place called Eathie, there used to be a mill, near which the fairies used to gather to dance. People knew of the magic powers of the fairies and it was generally thought a good idea to keep out of their way whenever possible. It was understood that fairies could give great gifts but they weren't human and no human could ever fathom their ways. They might do good or they might do harm; the best way of avoiding trouble was to avoid them altogether.

Now, the miller at Eathie lived in a house close enough to the mill to hear it turning at night. He knew it was the fairies grinding their own meal. They had been doing it since his father's time and *his* father's time before him, and the miller just accepted it as part of the way things were and never let it bother him. They didn't bother him, so he wouldn't bother them. It was a case of letting sleeping dogs lie.

One night the miller was in the local tavern with a couple of friends of his: the local piper Tam MacEashan and John Mackay, a farmer. It would hardly be stretching the truth to say that they had had a glass or two.

Tam was feeling a bit fired up with the drink and brought up the subject of the fairies.

'Are they still using your mill at nights then?' he asked the miller.

'Aye, that they are, but you know that it disnae bother me in the least. They aye leave the place neat and tidy and, as lang as they dinnae bother me, I'll just let them be,' said the miller in reply.

'Does it not bother you that they are using the mill and no paying you a penny piece?' asked Tam, a bit forcefully.

'Ach. Caw canny, Tam, ye ken fine that they've aye ground their meal at night. It's been the way of things for generations. Why try an' sort something that isnae broken?' said Mackay.

'Well, I think that you are aw scared o the fairies; I'm no scared of them and in fact I tell you what I'll do – I'll bet ye a bottle o the finest whisky that I can spend the night in your mill, playin my pipes for the wee folk and come out in the morning fit as a Fiddle,' He smiled at his companions, pleased with the idea of playing for the fairies. 'I'm pretty certain they'll aw be glad to hae a wee dance when I start playin.'

Now, the farmer and the miller tried to dissuade the piper from going to the mill, but seeing they were all a wee bit the worse for wear with the whisky, they soon began to think it might not be a bad idea. In truth, they thought the piper would last about twenty minutes and come running from the mill, so they decide to humour him. Tam went home to get his pipes, then was accompanied to the mill by his two friends. By now it was dark, but when they got to the mill there was no activity.

'Just you leave me here now,' said the piper, and the two friends left him and went back to the tavern. As they went they could hear the piper beginning to play. It was his favourite tune, 'The Haughs o Cromdale'. They were sure he would soon get fed up and come along to join them at the inn.

However, there was no sign of him after an hour, or even two hours. By this time the miller and the farmer had had a lot of whisky and both went straight home to get a good night's sleep before work in the morning.

In the morning, Mackay came to the mill just as the miller got there. The door of the mill was open. They went in. The fire was still set but hadn't been lit; the contents of the log basket had been spilled all across the floor. But of the piper there was no sign. Thinking that he had simply gone home from the mill rather than joining them at the inn as they had thought he would, they smiled at each other and went about their business. Later on in the day Mackay went round to the piper's house. The door was locked and there was no sign of him. He looked into the tavern and asked everyone he met, but no one had seen the piper since the night before. So he headed back to the mill and told the miller he couldn't find Tam.

'Now that is a bit strange,' mused the miller. 'He's certainly no in the mill.'

'Well, he had a fair bit to drink; maybe he fell asleep in the auld barn,' said Mackay.

So they looked in the miller's barn, but again there was no sign of their friend. They were now getting a bit worried so decided to look around the area, splitting up to do so. An hour later they came back to the mill and neither had any news at all of the piper.

'Well, maybe the fairies did get him. What do you think?' the miller asked Mackay.

'Well, I dinnae ken one way or the other, but I am worried for him,' replied the farmer. 'Look, I tell you what I'll do. I'll take a turn in the mill tonight just to see if I can find anything out. What do you think?'

The miller looked a bit dubious. 'If you're sure now. What if you disappear as well?'

'Och, I'll be careful. I just need to know what happened to Tam,' came the reply. 'I'll bar the door; if anybody but Tam comes by I'll just no let them in.'

The miller reluctantly agreed to this, and that very same night Mackay made his way to the mill. He barred the door, lit the fire in the grate and sat himself down to wait.

It seemed to him that it wasn't long after darkness fell when he heard piping outside. He recognised the tune. It was 'The Haughs o Cromdale' – Tam's favourite. And he recognised the piping. It was Tam. He hurried to the window and looked out; there he saw a crowd of fairy dancers and beyond them, half-hidden in shadow, was Tam. Suddenly there was a loud knocking on the mill door. Mackay ignored it. The knocking came again and he moved over beside the fire. At that, the door flew open, the bar holding it shut flying through the air to land at the far end of the mill. In came a wee man dressed all in green, with sharp, pointed features.

'And who are you?' he demanded in a shrill, loud voice.

Mackay, aware of the danger he was in, grabbed a burning brand from the fire and said to the fairy in Gaelic, 'Mi fhim is mi fhim (I am myself),' and thrust the brand into the face of the fairy. The wee creature let out a terrible scream and ran back out into the night.

Hearing the noise, the fairies all stopped dancing and clustered round their companion, who was moaning in agony and holding his hands to his face.

'Who did this to you?' demanded several of them at once.

'Mi fhim is mi fhim,' replied the fairy between sobs.

At that the fairies all burst into hoots of laughter.

'Well, we can hardly help you if you did that to yourself,' came the reply. Mackay was watching carefully round the edge of the window and wondering what would happen next. The piping had stopped and there was no sign of Tam. Just then, to his total surprise, a cock crew nearby and the fairies scattered like leaves in the wind. In less than a second there wasn't a creature to be seen before the mill. No fairies, and not a sign of Tam either.

That night in the tavern was a gloomy one. Mackay told his tale and all there realised that Tam had in truth been spirited away by the fairies. However, the farmer's quick thinking was noted and complimented and several drinks were taken, in relative silence, in honour of their lost friend, Tam the piper.

Tam was never seen by a human again. But if, on a moonlit night, you pass by where the fairies used to grind their corn at the mill of Eathie, you can sometimes still hear him playing his favourite tune for the little folk.

Robin Og and the Fairy Pipes

Robin Og lived near Loch Morlich, in the shadow of the Cairngorms, a part of the country much loved by the fairies. As a young man he had often seen them as they played and danced on the hills around Glenmore. Robin had been entranced by fairy music and, as he grew older, he himself learned to play the pipes. No matter how hard he tried he was never as good as he wanted to be. He often thought of how enchanting the music of the fairies was and how he had so longed to play like them when he was a child. Robin became a renowned hunter and news of his skill at tracking and taking the deer spread all over Strathspey. He was well-liked and highly thought of, but still in his heart of hearts he ached to play the fairy music. He was so taken with this idea that he hardly even noticed the looks he got from the young lasses of the area, many of whom thought he would be a good match. At long last, he decided that what he must do was steal a set of fairy pipes. Then some of their magic would rub off on him and he would become the great piper he had always wanted to be. So, knowing how the fairies often danced above Loch Morlich, he spent many nights on the hill waiting for a fairy dance to start. At last he was lucky. He came across a fairy piper playing away like anything for a group of his companions. Robin set himself down to watch and wait. For what seemed like hours he sat entranced, watching the little people dance like gossamer on the tops of the grass to the sound of the fairy pipes. At last, the fairy piper stopped and put down his pipes. Robin saw his chance. Springing forward, he snatched up the tiny bagpipes in his left hand, throwing his bonnet at the fairy and crying, 'Fair exchange, my mannie, fair exchange!' Without hesitating, he ran flat-out down the hill, not stopping till he had put more than a mile between himself and where the fairies danced. At last, breathing hard and red in the face, he opened his hand to see his treasure. There, nestling in the palm of his hand, was a dried-up puffball mushroom and three stalks of grass. Imagine thinking he could put one over on the fairies! Robin realised how daft he had been and from then on was a much happier man, finding himself a lovely young wife. In the fullness of time they were blessed with a bonny bunch of bairns, who loved to dance around the door of their house with their father playing his pipes.

The Pipers in the Pass

There are stories from all over Scotland about phantom pipers.

Some people have said they are due to the wind howling through telegraph wires, or even through trees, and others have suggested that they are simply imagined. The fact that they come from so many different areas suggests that the idea of the phantom pipers is one that has had a hold on the popular imagination for a very long time. The following story is from Rennie McOwan's *Magic Mountains* and it suggests that, as always, there is sometimes much more to some of our ancient stories than is often believed. It also suggests that scientific answers cannot always be found.

There has long been a tale of a phantom piper in the Corrieyarrick Pass between Strathspey and Fort Augustus in the Great Glen, which runs from Inverness to Fort William. This route has been used since long before any records were kept; it remained a significant passage through the hills till the time the British government set General Wade to building modern metalled roads through the Highlands in the 1730s. Over the years there have been many reports of people seeing phantom pipers here; it is suggested they may have something to do with the Highland army that marched south under the Marquis of Montrose to battle with the Covenanters at Inverlochy in 1645. Rennie McOwan makes a strong case for this being unlikely and suggests it was more likely the Highland army of 1745/6, which marched from the Great Glen to Ruthven Barracks in Strathspey. However, given that the Highlands were the scenes of cattle-raiding and battles between different clans over many centuries, the truth of the matter will probably never be known. It is a story that the rational-minded amongst us might tend to put down to the human imagination. But even rational-minded people should realise that there are some things that cannot be explained.

In 1958 a troop of Cameron Highlanders, mainly lads doing their National Service, were on a winter training exercise that was to take them eighteen miles, from Fort Augustus, through the Corrieyarrick Pass to Garranmore, just by Laggan in Strathspey.

It was March, but as is so often the case at this time of year in the Scottish Highlands, the snow still lay on the ground and the weather was cold, wet and windy. With the groups there were three pipers, and as they headed off towards the Corrieyarrick they played away quite merrily. However, the weather was against them: the haar, or freezing mist, settling down around the 300-metre mark. The route was uphill for about nine miles and, as they progressed, the weather got steadily worse. Snow began to fall and soon it became impossible to keep on playing in the cold, damp conditions. In fact, as the visibility weakened it became necessary for the soldiers to hang on to the kilt of the man in front to avoid going off the route. Up at the front something very strange was happening as they continued their ascent. Visibility at the front was no better than at the rear and, with everything covered in drifting snow and hardly any visibility, the two soldiers at the front were in extreme danger of losing the path. In front of them, however, were a pair of ptarmigan, the highland grouse that turn white in winter. They kept hopping and hovering in front of the men but still going forward. The soldiers kept their eyes on the birds and followed them, with the rest of their detachment coming up behind them, each man holding on to the kilt of the man in front. The men behind them had no idea of this till later.

At last, the birds crested the hill and the lead soldiers soon realised they had started their downward journey. Though there was still nine miles of terrible marching ahead, they knew it was downhill from here. All at once the ptarmigan disappeared. Needless to say, by this time the pipers had long given up playing and were struggling along like the rest.

At last they were nearing Garranmore and the officer in charge felt a great sense of relief. He was looking forward to a cup of hot tea and a hot meal, but knew that even after they got to the depot they would all have to wait for something hot to eat and drink. There was no radio at the depot and no word had been sent to inform the quartermaster sergeant at Garranmore of their imminent arrival. You can imagine the troop's surprise when they arrived at the depot to find the quartermaster and his men awaiting them with pots of tea and great pans of steaming stew.

'How did you know we were coming?' asked the incredulous officer.

'Och, we heard your pipes coming down the glen a while back, sir,' replied the quartermaster.

'Sergeant, our pipers haven't played a note since the other side of the pass – hours ago.'

'But we all heard them, didn't we, lads?' said the quartermaster, turning to the other men of his squad. They all agreed that they had heard the pipers and that was why they had prepared the meal.

'I'm a piper myself, sir,' said the quartermaster, 'and I know what I heard.'

The meal was soon over and the entire detachment moved on to the next stage of their training as quickly as possible.

In ancient Highland tradition there was a belief that the ptarmigan was the mother of all birds and capable of giving protection to humans. Whatever happened on the Corrieyarrick that day had plenty of witnesses – but no explanation.

The Lure of the Fairy Pipes

There was a man in Brevig village on the isle of Barra who was awful fond of beachcombing. He was fascinated with the endless supply of strange, and sometimes valuable, things he found washed up along the shores of Barra. In those olden times, before the advent of radar and other such new-fangled inventions, shipwrecks were much more common; useful items were often washed up. One day, the breachcomber was at Port an Duine on the lookout because the wind was blowing in from sea and he thought there could be various bits and pieces. Half the fun of the beachcombing was precisely that you never knew what you were going to find. Anyway, this day all he found was a piece of human jaw, with the teeth still in it. He picked it up and looked at it, but he felt his skin crawl so he threw it away.

After wandering along the beach for a while and finding nothing of interest, he decided to head back home. He had just got into the grassy area behind the beach when he heard pipe music. He realised that whoever the piper was he was pretty good, so he looked around to see where the piping was coming from. It was coming from beneath a large stone in the grass. Intrigued by this, he lifted up the stone, which was a lot easier than he thought it would be, and underneath the stone he saw a flight of stairs. So down the stairs he went and into a room, following the sound of the pipes. There was the piper, an old grey-headed man in beautiful green Highland dress with silver-buckled shoes. The room was cosy, with a fire burning on one wall. When the old man saw him, he stopped playing and invited the beachcomber to have a bite to eat.

Now, he was a bit reluctant as he didn't know who the old fellow was, but to keep him happy he shared the man's food. He wasn't impressed at all by the food he was given. After only a little while the old man made it clear that he should leave and told him to put the stone back exactly as it had been when he left. So he shrugged and headed back up the stairs. He put the stone back exactly as he had found it, then headed home, noticing that the wind that had been blowing earlier had died down and it was a warm sunny day.

When he came over the rise above his cottage he got an awful shock. There was his cottage right enough, but the roof had fallen in and the whole place was covered in nettles and bracken. He stood there utterly at a loss as he looked around. Then he saw another house not far off and, walking as if in a dream, he headed there. The door of the house was open; sitting just inside was a man making a pair of shoes. From his deft movements and practised use of the tools, it was obvious that the man was a cobbler to trade. He knew of no cobbler living here, or anywhere nearby at all.

'Come in, stranger,' said the cobbler. 'Have a seat and a drink of water; it's a hot day.'

'Aye, that it is,' replied the man, unsure of what to say, or of what was going on.

As soon as he had had a drink, he told the man that he had been walking out round Ru Mor and Port an Duine when he met the old man in the underground house. The cobbler looked at him long and a bit strangely. He moved as though to speak, but stopped. Then, as if summoning up some inner strength, he took a deep breath and said, 'Well, I remember a story my great-grandfather told me about an old fellow hereabouts who went missing after he had gone for a walk on the beach. He was a bit of a beachcomber; everyone assumed that he had gone into the sea after some driftwood or something and had been swept away. He was never seen again.'

At this, the man realised that he had been lured away by the charm of the fairy pipes. He sat himself down and the cobbler saw that the old man was suddenly weary to his soul. At once he got one of his children, who were playing round the back of the house, to go off to Eoligarry on the north of the island to fetch the local priest. When the priest came, the man knelt to receive his blessing outside the cobbler's house. As soon as the priest spoke, the old beachcomber crumbled away to dust and the wind whipped the dust away.

The Piper of Keils

All over Scotland, people knew that the fairies lived in mounds; in many areas stories were also told that the little people lived in caves. One of the caves where people thought they lived was at

Keils, at the southern end of the Mull of Kintyre. It was believed locally that there were long winding passages running far inland from the cave; deep within the earth at the end of the tunnels was the great hall of the fairies, lit by thousands of fairy tapers and ringing with the sound of a thousand fairy musicians. Here they would hold their revels, with their queen sitting over them all, and here she would pronounce judgement on any mortal daft enough to enter. People tended to keep clear of the cave, for it was common knowledge that the fairies had serious powers and were vengeful if affronted. Nobody knew what would or would not affront the little people, but they were known to be extremely touchy about all sorts of things. It was generally thought best to keep well away from them at all times. So people just avoided the cave.

At the time there was a piper called Alasdair living in nearby Keils. He was a brave lad and well known for his piping skills. He was the local blacksmith and every evening after his stint at the smiddy he would play his pipes. He loved the old tunes he had learnt as a child and was always looking for more. Any musician that came to the area would soon meet Alasdair, who would always try to pick up new material. He was also keen on playing for people whenever he could and many a convivial night was spent in the inn at Keils with Alasdair playing his pipes. Now, although he was young, he wasn't that young, but he had never taken himself a wife. He was always telling people that there was plenty of time for settling down once he had a bit more in the bank. His constant companion was a wee Border terrier called Sandy. The dog went everywhere with him and seemed to love the piping. In fact, it would be fair to say that they were devoted to each other, dog and piper.

Now, being a blacksmith, Alasdair was a strong man and this, combined with youth, meant he considered himself to be afraid of nothing. One night in the pub, round the fire with his friends, the talk turned to the little people – the fairies.

Mention was made of the fact that the fairies were great ones for music and that they had their own pipers and fiddlers, who had access to music that was far beyond the skills and abilities of mere humans to master. Someone told the story of the MacCrimmons getting their music from the fairies in the first place, and all agreed that their otherworldly music was supposed to be truly magical.

Alasdair had been sitting listening to this, turning his glass of whisky round and round in his hands.

'Well,' he said, 'ye all seem tae think that the fairy pipers are the very best. I'm not so sure and I tell you what I'll do – I'll pipe ye a tune as good as any that's played.' The company all looked at him and one or two eyebrows were raised.

'And what is more,' said Alasdair, intent on making his point to all there, 'I'll play it in the great cave down at the shore.'

'Now, now, Alasdair,' said Jamie McEacharan, 'just be careful what ye're saying. There's no need to take the risk of upsetting the wee folk. Ye ken fine what they can be like.'

'Aye, Alasdair,' put in Willie Kyle, 'dinnae be daft. That's an unco place that cave. Ye nivver can be sure what'll happen if ye go in there. An, as for piping, weel that would just be like a red rag tae a bull tae the fairies.'

The others round the table all agreed and told Alasdair that he would be daft to attempt such a feat.

Iain McGraw, a local farmer, said, 'Now, Alasdair, nobody disputes ye're the finest piper in all o Kintyre, but ye're jist human. Ye ken the fairy music; ye cannae match the magic music o the little people. It is said they can charm the birds from the trees or a man fae his ain true love . . .'

'Aye,' interjected Michael Doyle, 'my granny told me they could turn the love o a babe from its mother wi their playin.'

All were agreed that Alasdair, grand piper though he was, should forget about what he had just said.

But Alasdair was young and headstrong and stood up to

declare: 'Well, I'll bet I can play right through the pathways o the auld cave and come oot again as no fairy will challenge *my* piping wi a sweeter tune or better playing . . .'

At that, he picked up his pipes and burst into 'The Nameless Tune'. He played it brilliantly – nobody could argue with that – but try as they might to discourage him from going ahead with his plan, Alasdair was adamant. He would play in the great cave and let the fairies hear what a human piper could really do.

Now, the little folk are wise in many ways and have uncanny abilities in hearing and seeing. So it was that they heard of this boast and, deep in the cave, the thousand minstrels who played there for the elf queen herself soon knew of Alasdair's intention. The insolence of the piper was noted and, with the permission of the fairy queen, they prepared an enchantment for the foolhardy piper. All this was happening just as Alasdair was playing back in at the inn, for, truth be told, fairy time is not as we know time.

The more his friends tried to dissuade him; the more stubborn Alasdair became. At last he said, 'I'm going to do it, no matter what you say. In fact I'm going to do it right now.' Picking up his pipes, he headed for the door and struck up a tune as he headed towards the beach and the cave. For once in his life the wee dog Sandy delayed following his master, and, as if sensing something was going wrong, he growled deep in his throat before scurrying off after the piper.

As the piper headed off, blowing all the way, his friends followed him from the inn towards the beach, still calling on him to stop. Some of them were sure that, once he got to the cave, Alasdair would see sense and not tempt fate any further. On and on he went.

They came to the cave and the companions all held back. Not so Alasdair. Stopping only to gather his breath, he turned and smiled at the small group of his friends and neighbours before putting the mouthpiece to his lips, striking up 'The Nameless Tune' and heading jauntily into the cave, with his faithful wee dog at his heels. Within seconds he had disappeared into the darkness of the cave playing brightly. Iain McGraw said, 'I wish I were wrong, but I tell you that's the last we'll see of our Alasdair.' A couple of the others nodded in agreement. Still they could hear the piping, though it seemed to be very far off. Then the sound would soar and it was if he was near the mouth of the cave. This went on for a while. Then all of a sudden the piping turned to a wild squeal. Then there was silence. Suddenly the silence was split by echoing eerie laughter; then silence returned.

The men on the beach looked at one another. They knew something dreadful had happened, but maybe, just maybe, if no one spoke, it would be all right. They were all still standing looking from one to another and into the mouth of the great cave when a scrabbling noise came from the darkness within. All stepped back. Then the wee dog Sandy flew out of the mouth of the cave – not a hair was left anywhere on his body and he ran from the cave as if the red-eared hounds of hell were at his heels.

There was no sign of Alasdair. They waited till dawn and called into the cave again and again. Each and every time one of them tried to go more than a few feet inside, it was as if they could hear the uncanny laughter again and their blood ran cold. Try as they might, none of them could bring themselves to go into the cave. It was as if there was an invisible barrier beyond which it was impossible for them to pass.

So they returned to their homes. Within a day, the entire peninsula had heard what had happened to the bold piper – though maybe foolish would be a better word. Everyone was shocked, but as much at Alasdair's reckless bravery as at his disappearance. People just knew you could not hope to cross the fairies and get away with it. He maybe hadn't asked for such a gruesome fate, but he had gone into the cave of his own free will.

A while later Iain MacGraw was sitting with his wife by the fire when she knelt down and put her ear to the hearthstone.

'What is it, love?' he asked.

'Can't you hear it? Come down here,' she replied.

He knelt down and put his ear to the hearthstone. Faintly but clearly he heard it. It was a bagpipe and the piper was playing 'The Nameless Tune'. They knew it was Alasdair, doomed by the little folk to wander for all eternity through the underground passages of the cave, playing the same tune till the end of time. They thought they heard the tune stop for a bit and a far-off echoing sound of Alasdair's voice crying in anguish, 'I doubt, I doubt, I'll never win out. Ochone for my ageless sorrow.'

And there are those that say to this day that if you stand long enough where Iain MacGraw's croft used to stand you will hear the doomed piper and maybe even his desperate cry.

The Chisholm's Black Chanter

Now, in Scotland's history there have been several men who have devoted their lives to the study of the black arts. The best known is probably Michael Scott the Wizard, though there were others, such as the Wizard Laird of Skene, who had a peculiar pact with the devil. Another of this type was Chisholm of Strath Glass in Invernessshire, whose home was Erchless Castle. From a young age he had been fascinated by magic and the supernatural and, even though he got married and settled down, he couldn't seem to lose his fascination with the occult.

So, only a year or so after his marriage, he decided to go off to Italy, where he had heard there was a great master of the black arts who was prepared to take pupils. After more than six months, his wife began to get worried. There was no sign of her husband and she had received no word from him. She grew more and more worried and asked around the clan for someone to go after him. None of the Chisholms fancied going; if something had happened to their kinsman who was adept in the ways of magic, what chance could they have in going after him?

However, there was one man who came forward to offer his help. This was the local piper, a man by the name of Cameron, who had often played for Chisholm and felt beholden to him. So he was dressed in hodden gray instead of the tartan plaid, and given a sum of money and detailed instructions as to where he should go and what to do. He then set off after Chisholm to Italy.

After many troubles (his Gaelic was good but his English poor, and his knowledge of French and Italian non-existent), he at last came to the town in Italy where his master was supposed to be. He had made it all the way using sign language and showing people the name of the town he was looking for. Along the way he had made himself a bit of money by playing the pipes, though in more than one village he had been chased by dogs when the locals objected to the best of Scottish music. And, sure enough, the pipes are not to everyone's taste.

He arrived early one Sunday morning at the town and figured, as it was a small place, the best place to find the Chisholm would be the church. The church was pretty full when he got there so he went in and sat in a prominent chair near the door.

Now, he didn't know it, but this was the chair of hospitality, where people who had fallen on hard times could sit and everyone passing would give them something. As he sat there, half asleep in the warm Italian heat, he didn't notice that the service was over. Everyone who passed him dropped a coin in the bonnet he was holding in his lap. And at last the Chisholm himself came by and dropped a coin. Realising that he had found him, Cameron quickly pocketed the cash that was in his bonnet and ran to catch up with the Chisholm.

'Hello, sir, it's me, Cameron the piper,' he called as he caught up with Chisholm.

'Good Heavens, man, whatever are you doing here?' replied Chisholm, clearly startled to see the piper there in Italy.

'Mrs Chisholm has sent me, sir,' Cameron went on. 'She is worried sick to death not having heard from you. She sent me to see if you were all right and to ask you to come home,' he continued.

'Well, that's as may be,' said Chisholm, giving Cameron a funny look. 'But we'll have to see about this. Follow me,' he said, turning on his heel and walking away from the church. Cameron followed as he was told and they soon came to a great house with massive iron gates. Chisholm gave them a little push and the two great doors swung open to reveal a courtyard. Through this they hurried and on into the house. Cameron followed Chisholm up a flight of stairs and along a corridor, where he stopped outside a door and knocked.

'Vene,' came a deep voice from behind the door. Chisholm went in and signalled for Cameron to follow him. There sat an old man in a black robe on a vast great throne, with a dog at his feet and, sitting on an arm of his throne, a great black bald-headed bird the likes of which Cameron had never seen before. The room was filled with a heavy cloying scent and Cameron began to fill a little dizzy.

'Ah, well,' croaked the man in a voice that sounded as old as time itself, but in clear English, 'a visitor who has come a long way. Let me see.'

He raised his hands to his forehead and closed his eyes. Cameron was finding it difficult to breathe but Chisholm stood there calmly awaiting the words of the magician.

'Yes, I see now,' the old man said. 'You must go home, Chisholm. Your man here has filled his pockets, I see.' Saying that, he smiled and Cameron shivered. 'Yes, you must go home and I will help you. There is a strange man in your bed in Strath Glass!'

Chisholm's hand went to his sword in an involuntary movement and he blurted out, 'A strange man in my bed? Please master, can you help me get home quickly?'

And, so saying, he fell on one knee and bowed his head. The old magician looked at him, then glanced briefly at Cameron. The piper felt as though he had been flicked with fire.

'Mmm, yes, I can help you, Chisholm, but I want something from you first,' the old man croaked.

'Anything, master, anything you wish,' Chisholm burst out.

'Well, as you shall be going home rather quickly,' and the old magician smiled as he said that, 'you will have no further use for your magnificent black stallion, will you?'

'It is yours, master,' said the still-kneeling Chisholm. 'What must I do now?'

The wizard gave him explicit instructions. Chisholm was given a chanter by the old magician and the two Scots were sent off to the same bed as soon as night fell. There they were to take turns playing the chanter till morning, until they heard the cock crow. Chisholm told Cameron to do just as he was instructed and that all would come clear later. By the time the cock crew both men were exhausted and, despite their best intentions, fell fast asleep.

Cameron awoke to the sound of a laverock singing, high in the sky above. Before opening his eyes he sniffed the air. There was a smell of pine all around him. He opened his eyes and sat up just as Chisholm stirred. Looking around, Cameron realised they were in Ross Wood, between Erchless Castle and the River Glass. He lay there stunned; Chisholm leapt to his feet, drawing his sword, and running off towards the castle.

Cameron got to his feet rather groggily and ran after Chisholm. He was in a state of confusion but realised he had better be there when Chisholm confronted the stranger who was sleeping with his wife.

Through the wood they ran and straight into the castle. The great iron yett, or gate, lay open but Cameron hardly gave it thought. Everything was strange and the thought passed through his mind that he was dreaming. By now Chisholm was running up the stairs to the second floor, three at a time, and Cameron tried to catch up.

Along the corridor Chisholm ran and, without a second's hesitation, burst into the main bedroom.

He had just entered the room when he came to dead stop and Cameron, running up behind, tripped over him, almost knocking Chisholm over. Cameron lay on the floor and looked up at Chisholm. There he stood, sword in hand and his jaw hanging loose. Getting to his knees, Cameron looked over the edge of the bed. There, just coming awake, was Chisholm's wife and beside her lay the strange man – a lovely wee baby boy. It was only as he noticed this that Cameron became aware he was still holding the black chanter.

As the lady of the house came to, she was overjoyed and relieved to see her husband standing there. As for Chisholm himself, he was speechless. He had a son. His wife had not been unfaithful at all; she had just presented him with a son and heir. The celebration that followed was one to shake the rafters right enough, and Cameron was guest of honour at the event.

The black chanter that had somehow flown the pair of them all the way from Italy also had other properties. The master had told Chisholm that whenever there was to be a death in his family the chanter would crack. As long as it was repaired with a band of silver it would still function as well as ever. And what had been foreseen came to pass and the chiefs of the Chisholms all came to treasure the magical gift from the old wizard.

During the Jacobite Rising of 1715 what had been Cameron the piper's house was burned down by government troops. Cameron himself had lived out his days by Erchless Castle and had been succeeded as the Chisholm piper by his son and then grandson, who was living there at the time. When the then chief of the Chisholms heard that the piper's house had been burned down he got on his horse and raced down to Moot Hill, the traditional meeting place of the clan in times of trouble or great events. Thomas Cameron the piper was standing on the top of the knoll, looking out into the glen.

Chisholm dismounted and ran up to him. 'What of the black chanter, Thomas? Is it all right?' the chieftain quickly asked.

Turning to him, Thomas smiled, patting the set of pipes tucked under his arm. 'Here it is, sir; we lost everything but the pipes,' he said with a sad smile.

'Give me the chanter,' said Chisholm and the piper detached it from the bagpipes and handed it over.

Turning it over in his hands, the chief began to extemporise a song. And as he sang he danced, holding the chanter in the air. And these are the words he sang, though the original was of course in Gaelic:

Black chanter of my great grandsire
I rejoice that it is in my hand
I care not for all the fire got
Since the chanter is not there
I care not for what was burnt
I care not for what was lost
I care not for what was burnt
Since the chanter is not there.

And that was the origin of the reel, 'The Chisholm's Black Chanter', which was long very popular in and around Strathglass.

As was the way of things in those days, the whole of the clan gathered to help Thomas build a new home. The man who did not add a new stone to his house added a rafter, as the saying has it. When the house was rebuilt, a barrel of the finest whisky was brought down from Erchless Castle and Thomas played the new tune that the chief had composed. Then every man there took out his purse and by the end of the day Thomas Cameron, the piper of Clan Chisholm, was wealthier than he had been before.

A few months later Thomas had been playing at a wedding in Comar. It was a grand affair, with a great many gifts from the community to the new couple to help set them up. But most important of all was that Thomas Cameron was there to play the music. He was in the middle of playing a reel for all the gathered people after the ceremony, when the assembled company heard a loud crack and Thomas stopped playing. Even though it was a wedding and music was needed they could not get Thomas to play any more. Another chanter was brought, and even another set of pipes, but all he would say was, 'It is time for me to go back to the castle.' So he wrapped up the pipes in a fold of his plaid and left the wedding party. Another piper was encouraged to take over and the celebrations continued, but there were those who also left at that point, for they knew what the cracking sound had been. The black chanter had cracked under Thomas's fingers, and, on his return, he found the chief of Clan Chisholm laid out for burial. By the time of the funeral, Thomas Cameron had repaired the chanter with another band of silver and played his chief's coronach.

Today there are five silver bands round the Chisholm's black chanter, though some say others have fallen off.

The Spectre o Drummochter

The road through the heart of the Highlands from Perth to Inverness goes through the Pass of Drummochter, one of the highest roads in Britain. Here the weather can be grim and, when the snows fall in the depths of winter, hundreds, even thousands, of deer come down to shelter in the shadow of the two highest mountains, the Boar of Badenoch and the Sow of Atholl. This is also the setting for an eerie event that sometimes happens as the day shifts into the gloaming, that period of almost half-light before dusk comes on, when the magic of Scotland's landscape is at its strongest.

In 1746 the army of Prince Charlie was back in Scotland. A collective failure of nerve at Derby, when a concerted push to

London could have given them control of the capital, removed the last chance of success. Arguments had raged between the prince's advisers and his secretary, Murray of Broughton, probably had a strong influence on the eventual decision. In the light of Murray later deserting the Jacobite cause and joining the Hanoverians, the decision seems all the more decisive. Not that the army was in disarray. The defeat of the bumptious General Hawley, who had boasted of what his men would do to the Jacobite rabble, at Falkirk on 17 January showed they were still a formidable army. Again, however, a failure to follow up this victory was to cost the Jacobites dear. The prince wanted to harry the fleeing government troops and retake Edinburgh but, as a result of the combination of cautious advice and the departure of some of his troops, he let the opportunity pass. Many Highlanders, having gathered loot on their journey so far, wanted to go home to their homes in the glens and, as they had never been regular soldiers under strict military command, it was difficult to stop them doing this. The government troops had come under the control of the king's son, the duke of Cumberland, a man whose barbarity was to become known at Culloden and after.

The government troops greatly outnumbered the Jacobites, whose failure to raise more support in England was to cost them dear. From Falkirk onwards there definitely seems to have been a lack of clear ideas as to how to proceed. The Jacobite army itself split in two at Crieff after the battle of Falkirk: one section, under Lord George Murray, headed north along the Tay and up the coast; the rest of the troops, under the prince himself, headed towards Inverness through the Highlands. They passed by Dunkeld and Pitlochry and headed for the Drummochter pass to go on into Strathspey.

Cumberland, a despicable human perhaps, but a decisive and commanding soldier, had sent out cavalry to harry the Jacobite troops; by the time they had reached the Pass of Drummochter, the government cavalry were close upon them. One of the problems of having so many Highlanders in the Jacobite army was that they had their own ideas of how to fight. The fearsome Highland charge that had been so successful at Prestonpans and elsewhere arose from the particular style of the Highlander. They were not trained like soldiers: they were warriors, and the idea of obeying precise and strict orders was something they had difficulty with. So, when the prince ordered the rearguard of his army not to chase after the cavalry who were harrying the rear, there was some dissatisfaction.

The prince had a point, however. The government dragoons were fresh and well-supplied. The Highland troops had been on the march for months and were weary to the bone. They were also less well supplied than the troops attacking them. The legendary capacity of the Highland warriors to subsist on little more than a handful of oats and a tot of whisky stood them in good stead, but there are limits to human endurance. The Highlanders thought that the constant harrying and retreat of the troops of dragoons was an insult to their own fighting skills and many of them wanted to turn and attack the Hanoverian troops. At last, just as they got to Drummochter, a group of them decided enough was enough.

The rearguard of the army was mainly composed of MacDonalds and MacPhersons, who decided that they would resolve the situation themselves, despite the orders coming from the top. Six hundred of them resolved to attack the dragoons next time they came close.

So, as the cavalry came up and fired their guns at the rear of the Jacobites, they turned and charged. Immediately, the mounted troops wheeled round and galloped off. However, Highland warriors were not much slower than horses over the rough Highland ground and the officers of the Hanoverian troops soon realised they might not outrun the Jacobites. So the government troops came to a halt on a small hill and decided to make a stand. Seeing this, the Highland troops slowed down. Out came a dozen and more sets of pipes and they began to play a stirring march as the Highlanders got ready to charge. It was just after noon when they decided to attack. Now, the preferred use of the famous Highland charge was to run downhill, but here they would be running uphill. This meant nothing; they had made up their minds to wipe out the dragoons. As the Highlanders charged to the skirl of the pipes, they were subjected to withering fire from the entrenched troops above. The slaughter was horrific but the MacDonalds and the MacPhersons persisted. On and on they came, as the great pipes roared them on. They were in a do-or-die frame of mind and kept going till they were close enough for hand-to-hand fighting. In such a situation, the government troops were no match for the skilled sword and dirk play of the kilted warriors. Some tried to escape on their horses, but the Highlanders were well versed in how to deal with mounted troops; those few horses that were mounted were hamstrung and the riders stabbed to death where they fell. Once hand-to-hand combat started, the conclusion was inevitable. Not one of the government troops survived. The last of them managed to crawl off the hill and reached a nearby burn before he died. To this day, the burn carries the name Allt na Sassunaich, the Burn of the Englishman. (Actually, Sassunaich means a speaker of the Saxon tongue, but it is used generally of English people.)

The carnage that day was dreadful, with the sound of the pipes soaring over the cries of wounded and dying men, of hamstrung horses and of the hoarse battle cries of the triumphant clansmen. Even today, there are those who will tell you that if you walk through this part of the Pass of Drummochter as the gloaming comes on, you will hear the sounds of battle and, over them, the wild skirling sounds of the great war pipes of the MacDonalds and MacPhersons. Others will tell you that on many an occasion, as night falls, wraiths of those ancient warriors and their enemies can be seen there in the Pass of Drummochter.

Why The Seals Have No Ears

At Hougary on North Uist there lived a widow with just the one son. Now, he had a liking for the pipes and at every chance was off playing them. But, as he was her only son, the widow was always on at him to be helping with the croft or to be out in the boat fishing. His head was full of the piping, however, and he had little love for the hard work that it took to keep the croft going. All the neighbours thought the lad had the makings of a fine player and had encouraged him from the start. This upset his mother and, as she was reckoned locally to be a powerful witch, nobody wanted to cross her. So, one by one, the neighbours stopped asking the young lad in for a play; pretty soon he had nobody at all to be playing to. So he would wander off to the shore and there he would play his bagpipes to the only audience he could find – the seals. Now, everybody in the islands knows that seals love music and will come whenever it is played. The seals were lucky in this case, for indeed the lad was a braw piper, but they didn't know what they were letting themselves in for.

The lad's mother was getting angrier by the day with the fact that, any chance he could, her son would slip off from her sight. She resolved to find out where he was going. She knew fine well that she had frightened off all the neighbours, but thought that maybe one of them was trying to get one over on her by supporting her son. One day, when he thought she wasn't looking, he slipped out of the croft house with his pipes – he had done this a hundred times before – and headed straight to the beach. His mother, though, had been keeping an eye open for just this sort of thing, and she followed him out of the house in time to see him head off towards the shore to the south. Keeping her distance, she went after him. After a little while she heard the bagpipes starting up. Cold, black fury filled her heart. 'Just wait,' she thought to herself, 'just wait. I'll teach you to encourage this feckless lad of mine, whoever you are.'

She could hear the pipes getting louder as she approached the beach, keeping low. When she reckoned she was close enough she stood up, pointing her right forefinger ready to curse anyone there listening to her son. But there was not a human to be seen. Instead, there were hundreds and hundreds of seals lying along the beach all paying rapt attention to the fine pipe music they were hearing.

Using all her power, she shouted, 'Stop!' and even over his pipes her son heard it. He took the pipes from his lips and turned to see his mother standing above him, pointing her finger.

'You, get to the peats this instant and gather our fuel, you useless gomeril,' she cried in a voice that would take no disobedience. The laddie stuck his pipes under his arm and ran past his furious mother towards the peats. He knew fine what her temper was like and had no intention of waiting about to catch the edge of her tongue.

As he ran off she turned to the seals assembled along the beach. Raising both her hands, she sang a song of imprecation in an old language long forgotten by all but the witches. But we know yet what she said:

I have had my say
that none should help and
that none should hear;
Now from this time
there is no seal
that shall have ears.

And that is why to this day seals have no ears.

The Ghost Pipers

There is a tale told by Ronald Douglas in *The Scots Book* that hints at many things. He lived on a croft in the hills near Ben

Wyvis in Easter Ross. The house sat beside a deep wooded gully, through which ran a burn called An Allt Mor, and above it were two rounded hills. On several occasions, both inside and outside the house, he heard the sound of pipes in the distance. Something about the sound was not quite right but he could never put his finger on it. A piper himself, he thought long and hard about it. Eventually he realised what the problem was – the pipes he was hearing were two-drone, not three-drone pipes! Now, the third drone on the pipes, the bass drone, had become standard by the seventeenth century – but he had played a set of two-drone pipes in Ireland on a visit once. So who could be playing such old-fashioned pipes up there in the hills? There were no nearby houses in that direction and he knew most of the people in the nearest glens; none of them, as far as he was aware, owned a set of two-drone pipes. The matter continued to puzzle him for quite a while. Maybe because the sound was coming from a distance he just wasn't hearing the bass – but he thought this couldn't be right. He was so intrigued by the sound that he took every opportunity he could to ask people in the area if they knew of anyone with a set of two-drone pipes, or even any pipers at all. He soon found out that there wasn't another piper within miles of his home.

One day he went to the nearest town, Dingwall, and met the man who had had the croft before him. He mentioned hearing the pipes to the man.

'Och, aye,' he replied, 'I mind I used to hear the pipes sometimes, but nobody ever believed me. So you hear them too? Well, that's a bit of a relief,' he smiled.

'Aye, I hear them,' said Ronald. 'Sometimes in the daytime and sometimes in the evening, but I can't figure out where they are coming from. I've tried to convince myself it's just the wind in the trees or the rippling of the burn but I know I'm only fooling myself . . .'

'Aye, well,' said the other, 'we both know it's the pipes, but as to who it is playing them, that's a different matter.'

Ronald was pleased to have had some corroboration of his experience, but the pipes still occasionally played and he was no nearer to finding out why.

One night a month or two later – it was September time – he went out for a walk in the bright moonlight. This was the time of year the clans had traditionally raided each other under the light of the autumn moon; over to the north-east he could clearly see Ben Wyvis beyond the two knolls, or maman, above his croft house. Suddenly, there came the sound of a pibroch. It sounded close by, just over the ridge, but he decided there was no point in looking again for something that he was sure could not be seen. He listened for a bit and went home to bed.

Soon he was in a deep, troubled sleep. All at once, he sat bolt upright – moonlight was streaming in through the window and outside he could hear clashing noises and yells. It was the sound of metal on metal, sword on sword, accompanied by screams and yelling. It was an infernal din! Someone kept shouting out the same phrase in Gaelic, but, try as he might, he couldn't make it out. And, over all the noise, was the roar of the pipes, as many as a dozen sets all playing at full blast. The sounds were coming from the hill at the edge of the moor.

He was stricken with an unearthly fear; his skin turned clammy and sweat poured from his brow. However, he was an ex-perienced soldier and had seen some terrible sights in the First World War, so he was not going to be turned into a craven weakling by noises!

Up he got, pulling his kilt on over his pyjamas. Down the stairs he went, every hair on his head standing on end, but determined to find out what was going on. Suddenly the noises stopped. Then they started again, but this time it was something different. It wasn't the sound of battle but of marching warriors, the clatter of carried weaponry, shouts of victory and the pipes playing a victory march. Down the side of the burn the noises came, but out of the window there was nothing to be seen. On the noises came, then crossed over the burn and kept coming towards him. Then he heard another noise – it was his dogs, a bitch and her two five-month-old pups, whining pitifully from their cage. He went out of the house and let the dogs free. Off they dashed towards the noises on the moor. Within less than a minute they were back, running at full speed. The bitch stopped and curled at his feet, whining again, while the two puppies took off over the moor to return a few hours later.

On and on came the sound of the warband. As he stood at his barn door he heard the warriors come right past him – the creak of their swinging targes, the rubbing of metal on wood, the singing and shouting of victorious warriors, with the occasional higher-pitched tones of a woman among them – but not a thing was to be seen. And at their head were the pipers playing loud and clear in the bright moonlight – a victorious tune that felt very familiar, but which he did not recognise. He stood there as the band marched by him, straight through his house and away over the moor.

In the following days he thought he maybe understood a little of what had happened, for the hill over which the ghost army had appeared bears the ancient name Mam a Catha, 'the rounded hill of the battle'.

The Piper of Pontskinnen Pot

There was a piper in Glenesk by the name of Hamish Whyte, who was known through all the glens and Braes of Angus. He was a grand piper indeed and the fairies, who are always listening in to what humans talk about, became aware of him. People spoke of him so highly that the fairies decided to give him a listen themselves and were very impressed. As everyone knows, the fairies love to dance and have always been on the lookout for good musicians.

Now, Hamish liked to practice at a spot just by Dalbrack Bridge between the village of Tarfside and Loch Lee at the head of the glen. One evening he was playing away happily when a boat came down the River Esk. It was a strange-looking craft with a high prow and in it there were nine fairies all dressed in green, hooded robes. Hamish saw them coming out of the corner of his eye but decided to keep playing till he saw what was happening. The strange boat, with its even stranger crew, came to the bank of the river at the place called Pontskinnen Pot, just where the river widened a bit. The leader of the fairies stepped out of the boat and up the hill to where the piper was pacing up and down. Without a word being spoken, the fairy touched Hamish on the shoulder with a short white wand. She turned to go back to the boat and the piper followed her without losing a beat. Back down to the boat went the fairy and Hamish followed. Once they both were in the boat, the strange craft moved from the shore. Three times it made a circle in the broad stretch of the river at Pontskinnen Pot; then the craft headed up river. No one rowed, but the boat floated gently upstream towards the mountain of Craigmaskeldie at the head of Loch Lee. As the boat moved upstream the piper continued to play, the sound of his pipes becoming fainter and fainter as they went up the river and across the waters of the loch. There Hamish went with the nine fairies into a cave deep in the mountain and was seen no more. Sometimes, though, if you stand by the river beyond Tarfside you can still hear Hamish's pipes echoing in the wind coming down from the hills.

Glen Coe Piping

Of all the tragic stories told of Scotland's past – and there are many – perhaps the best known is the Massacre of Glencoe. In 1692, in the early hours of 12 February, MacDonalds were killed in their beds by troops sent amongst them on government orders. Some of them died in their beds; some tried to fight back, and many others froze to death after fleeing from the clachan. Much has been written about the abuse of Highland hospitality by the mainly Campbell troops billeted among the MacDonalds, and in truth the act was despicable. Traditionally, a guest was under the protection of his host and on many occasions this had brought trouble on the heads of those giving shelter to wanted men. However, the rules were clear and there were instances where men wanted by a clan were sheltered by members of that same clan, who had no option but to defend them. The Highland sense of honour may seem strange to us nowadays, but in the olden times the individual sense of honour was of major importance to every Highlander.

The massacre was carried out by troops under the control of Robert Campbell of Glenlyon, and he was carrying out government orders.

This was a horrific act, the news of which reverberated throughout Britain and helped to stoke up the Jacobite resentment that fuelled the later rebellions. However, although this blot on Scotland's history has been investigated time and again by historians, there are other stories that paint a somewhat different picture – a picture that puts Robert Campbell in a better light, if only just. It is said that while playing cards with MacIan, the venerable chief of the Glencoe MacDonalds, the evening before the massacre, Campbell had a fit of conscience. He knew what his orders were and, as a soldier, felt he had to follow them. But he was also of Highland birth himself and knew the horror his planned action would instil in people's hearts and minds. It might be he also thought the act so despicable he was looking for a way out.

Just after sunset he sent his piper round the houses where his men were billeted, all prepared for the bloody work ahead, to play the sunset call. He told the piper to play an old tune called

'Women of the glen take warning'. By this, the story goes, he hoped to warn the MacDonalds of the danger they were in. Much good it did. Where were the people of Glencoe to go, in the mist of a bleak winter, if they left their homes? Was he hoping the men of the clan would take up their arms and set about his own troops? It is said, however, that two of MacIan's sons heard the piping, recognised the tune and escaped under cover of darkness.

And More of Glencoe

After the atrocious slaughter at Glencoe, some of the Campbell troops headed back towards Fort Augustus. They were near Spean Bridge when suddenly they heard pipes being played up in the hills. The officer in charge was immediately suspicious and thought that it was one of the surviving MacDonalds summoning other survivors to him. So he ordered the troops to follow the piping. They headed into the hills; the piping got louder and louder the deeper they went into the hills, but always seemed to be round the next bend or behind a small hill in front of them. Eventually, they came to a dead end; there before them were the still black waters of a mountain lochan, its waters a sharp contrast to the snow-covered hillsides around it. Now, the Campbells were Highlanders themselves and there were mutterings about being led astray by a fairy piper, who had hoped to drown them in this lochan. Others thought it might have been the spirits of those they had so recently slain back in Glencoe. They were weary after their chase and there was no option but to head down the hill, back to where they had come from. Suddenly, on their way back down to the low ground, a child was heard crying. It was a pretty desolate spot and the officer realised that anyone carrying a child up there in this weather had to be a fugitive. He turned to the nearest soldier.

'Go find that child and shut it up. For good,' he ordered. So the soldier, a Lowlander, by this time in a state of near exhaustion himself, headed up the hillside to where they had heard the child crying. Behind him the rest of the troops carried on down the glen. As he half-staggered up to a small group of rocks, where he thought the child might be, he was stopped in his tracks.

A clear, beautiful woman's voice was singing an old Gaelic lullaby. It was the most beautiful and heart-breaking sound he had ever heard. It was the child's mother, totally exhausted but lulling her baby to sleep in the snow-clad mountains. And the soldier knew that she knew she was lulling it into its last sleep out here, far from any help in the freezing cold. Having fled all the way from Glencoe over the mountains in midwinter there was no chance they would survive. He walked on and over a little rise. The singing mother looked up at the red-coated figure standing over her with his sword in his hands. She didn't have the strength to move, lying there with her baby nestled deep into her breast. She spoke to him in that lovely voice, but she spoke in Gaelic. He was a soldier from the Lowlands and didn't have the Gaelic. But, as he stood there looking down on the pitiful sight, the thought came to him of his own wife and child back home. He remembered how he had last seen them, his wife waving goodbye with his tiny son standing at her feet. This was no job for a soldier. This was no job for a Christian man. The thoughts ran savagely through his head as the young woman looked up at him, the fear in her eyes turning to a blank look of acceptance.

Then he knew what he must do. He took the little rations he had from his wallet and handed them down to the woman. Her eyes brightened as she realised what was happening. Then he knelt, took off his greatcoat and wrapped it around her and the now sleeping child.

'Tapaidh leave, tapaidh leave,' she whispered, and he knew she was thanking him. His heart near to breaking, but knowing he could do no more, he ran off down the hill, his eyes blinded by tears. He came over a small rise; there in front of him was a wolf gnawing at the throat of another woman, dead, in the snow. With a howl of anger and anguish he swung his sword in both hands and sliced through the beast's head before it had time to move. A while later, shivering with cold, he caught up with the rest of his party. Showing the captain the bloodstained sword was enough. He didn't even mention the fact that the soldier had lost his greatcoat, so the soldier fell back among the troops and headed on towards warmth and food at Fort Augustus.

Some stories are told exactly as they happened, because they have to be, and others are sometimes told to lighten the horrors of life. But this story survives because the young woman in the snow survived, with her baby son, and for many years their descendants still walked the hills of Lochaber and passed the story of the magic pipes and the Lowland soldier down through the generations.

The Mermaid and the Piper

Down the centuries there have always been plenty people in Scotland wanting to play the pipes. Some manage fairly well; others take to it like naturals; and some folk never seem to get the hang of either the blowing of the mouthpiece or the fingering of the chanter. One such person was a young lad raised near Gairloch, called Ross. He badly wanted to play the pipes but, try as he would, he never could get the hang of it at all. Of course, if you are trying to learn the pipes you have to play a bit, but Ross's attempts at both the chanter and the pipes themselves drove his friends and family distracted. Eventually, after many months, his mother told him: 'If you want to practise the chanter or the pipes take them away down to the beach; you're driving us all daft here with your blowing and screeching.'

Now Ross realised that he had a problem, but he was a thrawn lad and was determined he would not give up. He intended to learn to play the pipes properly, no matter what effort it took. Having been sent off to the shoreline on his own to practise, he took to wandering along the coast, sometimes trying to play and sometimes not.

One day, having wandered a few miles up the coast from Gairloch, he caught sight of something on the rocks up ahead of him. He dropped down and looked over the edge of boulder. There, sitting on a rock, sunning herself, no more than two hundred yards from him was a mermaid! All at once he knew what he must do. He had never seen a mermaid before but he had heard enough about them to know what to do. He knew that if you managed to capture a mermaid she had to grant you a wish in order to be set free. So there and then he decided to capture this strange creature and demand a wish from her.

Now, although he was a stubborn, and maybe even a pig-headed kind of lad, he had always been good on the hill. He could creep up on game and birds like a fox. So down he got on his belly and began to inch his way along the edge of the beach, peeking over rocks and boulders and tufts of sea grass wherever he could. Closer and closer he got till he could hear the mermaid singing to herself as she lay on the rock in the sun. Slower and slower he went till he could just about reach out and touch her.

Then he sprang and grabbed her in his arms. At once she began to writhe and heave; he felt as if he was trying to hang on to a great slippery and strong eel. But he was determined. No matter how hard she wriggled he just gripped tighter; at last the creature gave up and lay in his arms. Then she lifted her head and looked him straight him the eye. He felt as if he was in a vast great echoing hall, where there was no sunlight.

'Right, human. What do you want of me?' she said, in a voice that echoed the breaking of the waves on the beach.

'If I let you go, will you give me a wish?' panted Ross, tired from wrestling this half-human creature.

'Well, you have managed to capture me right enough,' she

whispered. 'So I will promise to grant you a wish if you let me free.'

'Grand, grand. Aye, I have a wish to ask of you,' he said, finding himself intrigued by her half-human body and her long silvery hair, flashing in the sun like fish-scales.

'Well, then,' said the mermaid, 'you had better tell me what it is, hadn't you?'

'Aye, right,' he replied. 'What it is – I want to be able to pay the bagpipes,' he said, looking quizzically at her.

'Is it to please yourself or to please others you want to play?' she asked.

'Och, it's just to please myself,' he said. 'I have been trying so long and just can't get the knack of it.'

'Well then, you have my promise that as soon as you let me go you will be able to play the pipes,' she replied.

'Right then,' he asked, 'what do I do now?'

'Just let me go,' the mermaid replied.

At that, Ross released her she slid from his arms; into the water and disappeared. It was as if she had never been there. However, Ross realised that it was no dream – his clothes and upper body were wet.

At once he ran back to where he had first spotted the mermaid. There were his pipes. He bent down and stood up with them tucked under his arms. He placed the mouthpiece in his mouth, gave the bag a smack as he had seen real pipers do, and placed his fingers over the chanter as he began to blow.

Heavens above – he found he could play the tune he had been trying so hard to master that day. He played it once and once again. Then he tried another tune. He could play that as well. He was delighted and ran to the water's edge shouting, 'Thank you, thank you,' to the empty waves.

So Ross learned to play the pipes; there you would find him, down on the beach nearly every night, playing away to himself. For, true to her word, the mermaid gave him the gift of playing for himself – but anyone else coming near would always run away from the dreadful noise he made! It has long been said that the gifts of the fairies are not always what is expected.

The Lure of the Pipes

In Diebidale Forest in Easter Ross people used to think that the little people came out to dance in the winter on the tops of bogs, covered with ice so thin that even a wild duck could not cross without it breaking. The local head stalker, Big Jon, who lived at Clach-na-Harnich, was out one winter's night in the hills with his dog, Simon, and bitch, Bess, culling hinds. That night there was only a half moon and halfway up Corrie Glas he realised that the weather was on the turn. Clouds were beginning to scud in from the west and, knowing the hills as he did, he looked for a place to shelter from the blizzard he knew was on its way. Luckily, he soon found an east-facing cleft in the rocks, which opened up into a small cave. Here he wrapped himself in his plaid and hunkered down, with his faithful dogs snuggling into him, to wait out the storm. An hour or so later the snow stopped and, as there was just enough moonlight to see his way, he decided to take his chances and head home by Allt a 'Choin (the stream of the dogs) and the spot known as Poacher's Pool.

Now, Big Jon was a true Highlander and, like many another man who lived in the wild mountains, had a taste for whisky now and again. He was also very fond of the sound of the bagpipes. He was coming down the hill following Allt a 'Choin when, off to his right, he heard pipes playing 'Braham Castle', a tune he knew well. He realised that whoever the piper was he was making a fine job indeed of the tune. He was puzzled. He knew of no one living this far up on the mountain; surely no one would come out on a dangerous wild night like this just to play a few tunes in the hills. He decided to head towards the sound and, just as he did so, a cloud covered the moon. However, even in the near-dark, Big Jon could find his way and he carried on towards the sound of the pipes. He realised he was coming closer to the Poacher's Pool and at that point the pipes changed to a lively reel. Then, as he came over a small rise, he saw a light shining from the window of a wee cottage. This was where the pipes were being played, and played well indeed. Big Jon was suspicious – he had never seen this house before and realised something strange was going on. Still, this piping was better than any he had ever heard and seemed to be pulling him on. He felt he just had to find out who this wonderful piper was, no matter where he came from or who he was.

As he and his dogs neared the house, his black bitch sat down and refused to go on. Jon had seen this fine creature take on a full-grown stag and never flinch, but still the lure of the piping was working in him. 'All right, Bess,' he muttered to the bitch, 'just you stay here then. Simon will come with me. As long as I have him and Kisrule here,' he patted the gun under his arm, 'we have nothing to fear. Stay here, lass.'

At that, he headed straight to the cottage. Just as he was coming to the door he heard the tune change again, this time to 'Tullochgorum'; he had truly never heard such playing as this in his life. As he reached the door, it opened and there stood an old woman, a bit stooped and grey-haired but with clear shining eyes.

'Come in, come in, Big Jon, you'll be cold and hungry out there on the hill at this time of night. Come in, come in.'

Well aware that he was in a dangerous situation, Jon still wanted to hear more of the marvellous piping. He looked down at the old woman and asked, 'How do you know my name, mother?'

'Och,' she said, 'there isn't a body for twenty miles around here that doesn't know Big Jon, the head-stalker. Come on in, come on in.'

'Well, all right,' he said, 'I'll just come in for a minute to hear a tune or two.'

She stepped aside and in he went, hearing the door close behind him. Standing in the small lobby, Jon took off his bonnet; he was handing it to the woman when Simon jumped up and snatched it from his hand. The old woman seemed not to notice and opened the door to the kitchen of the cottage.

There before Jon was a real party. The room was filled with men and women – more of the latter – and every one of them was truly beautiful. They were wearing long frocks of a bluish-red, while the men all had frock coats and trousers with a greenish red sheen to them. They were truly a magnificent sight but Jon only had eyes for the piper. Standing by the bed closet at the far wall of the kitchen was big man, bigger even than Jon, clad from head to foot in full Highland dress. Jon looked but did not recognise the tartan at all; he noticed that the pipes had gold mounts and were as fine a set of pipes as had ever been made.

Again the tune changed to 'The Reel o Tulloch' and, as the brightly-dressed crowd danced and capered, Jon was sure that he saw sparks coming from the piper's fingers!

As the tune came to a close, the piper took the pipes from his mouth and looked at Jon with a smile, but didn't speak.

'Well, Jon,' said the old woman, who still stood beside him, 'will ye take a dram?'

John could only nod as a glass was poured and handed to him. He tossed it off without a word and by Jove it was good. He felt his whole body thrill to the power of the whisky; this was the real stuff indeed. The piper started up again with a schottische and a beautiful, tall, elegant lass took Jon by the hand and led him into the dance. They started the dance and Jon felt as if his feet were hardly touching the ground. The deep green eyes of the lassie whose hand he was holding seemed to reach deep inside him and a great smile of joy came onto his features. He moved to put down his gun, Kisrule, and take this gorgeous lass into his arms. Suddenly, there was Simon, his faithful dog, coming between him and the lovely young woman. He looked down to tell the dog to go away. And then he saw. Beneath the long blue and red gown he could see the lass's feet. Only they weren't feet but horse's hooves.

All at once, the spell was broken and he realised the danger he was in. He turned to see a malevolent red cloud beginning to seep out from under the closet door. He turned further to see the piper. There, in all his black power and fierce ugliness, was Auld Hornie. The piper was the very devil himself!

'God help me,' shouted Jon at the top of his voice. All around him the true nature of the formerly beautiful people was made manifest – devils and sprites, an ugly, wart- and canker-ridden crew from the shores of Hell!

The sound of the Lord's name gave the evil band pause, only momentarily, but Jon took his chance and leapt for the door calling, 'Come Simon, come.'

But the dog had other ideas and leapt straight at Auld Nick himself, who suddenly had a blood-stained rusty dirk in his hand; he pierced the animal to the heart as it leapt at him. Jon, realising he still had his shotgun, raised it and let fly with both barrels at the great black figure. The lead passed straight through the monster, who put back his head and gave a great laugh.

Jon, terrified to his very soul, took his chance and burst through the kitchen door, out the front door, into the snow and off into the hill. Behind him came the females, now in their true shapes, with flaming hair and blood-dripping fangs. They were only yards behind him. But Jon was a strong, fit man and headed for the Poacher's Pool. As he neared it, he looked over his shoulder. Four of the hags and Auld Clootie himself were only yards away. Deep in his heart Jon knew he was lost; but they would not get his soul. He would dive into the Poacher's Pool and drown himself. That way they wouldn't have him as their plaything for eternity. Just as he stood on the pool edge, about to jump, the devil was upon him and raised his dirk, still hot with the faithful Simon's blood, to strike Jon down. At that very moment a sound came on the clear night air.

'Cock-a-doodle-doo.' It was the cockerel down the glen at Rory's cottage. At once the awful denizens of hell disappeared, screaming in disappointment, and Jon, released from the effects of their malevolence, fell in a dead faint.

Several hours later he awoke with his dogs licking his face. Dogs? Surely Simon couldn't be here, he thought as he opened his eyes. Sure enough, there was the faithful and brave dog. Clutching the dogs to him in relief, he held Simon by the ears and stuttered out, 'Och, Simon, boy, I thought you were a goner. Thank the Lord for his help and thank you, you brave and faithful creature that you are; you have saved your master's life this night, and it will not be forgotten.'

Looking at the wonderful creature, he noticed for the first time that there in the dog's black chest were four single white hairs. Somehow, he knew not how, but somehow, he just knew that these hairs meant that the dog was safe against the power of the devil. And, thanking the Lord for the dog's sense and bravery, which had saved his life, Jon got to his feet and headed home. Jon kept Simon with him till the end of the dog's days, and on the nights they were out on the hill the both of them were watchful indeed.

There are those who will tell you that, even to this day, if you go up by Allt a 'Choin at night in winter you will hear wonderful piping by the Poacher's Pool in Diebidale Forest. But there aren't many prepared to give it a go.

A Royal Piper

➤◆◄

These two similar tales are part of a series of stories that have long been told about King James IV. It was believed that he regularly went about the kingdom in disguise, seeing how the people were getting on and keeping his eye on the barons and nobles who were supposed to help uphold the law. This might seem unusual behaviour for a king, but we should remember that Scottish monarchs were kings, and queens, of Scots, not of Scotland. It is stated in the 1320 Declaration of Arbroath that if the king did not do what was considered right he would be replaced by the 'whole community of the kingdom of Scotland'. It was also quite normal in medieval Scotland for people to address the king much as they would talk to each other.

A Piper and a Bully

Back in the Middle Ages there were powerful men who took the law into their own hands. One such was Sir James Tweedie of Drumelzier. He was in the habit of demanding tribute from all who crossed his lands, no matter how poor or how wealthy they were. Sir James and his armed men preyed on everyone in the area and those passing through. Now, one day, a lone traveller was heading through the hills towards Drumelzier when he heard the sound of the pipes. He hurried ahead and came in sight of a man playing the pipes as he walked along the road with his cow ahead of him. It looked as if he had put his cow out to pasture in the hills earlier and was now heading home. The piping was pretty good and the traveller ran to catch up with the man. He greeted him, telling him he was on the look-out for a place to stay that night.

'Och, that's no problem,' said the piper, whose name was Johnny Bartram. 'Just you come along wi me and you can stay with us tonight.' It turned out that, apart from being a piper, Bartram was also a cobbler. As was so often the case, he was rather poor; he owned very little land – in fact only enough to keep the one cow. He relied on shoemaking and piping to feed his family most of the time. Poor though he might be, he was well versed in the Scottish tradition of hospitality and that night the traveller had a grand time: singing songs, listening to the pipes and being fed plentifully, if plainly. In the morning breakfast was served – the usual staple of porridge, served up in wooden bowls with horn spoons – and the traveller tucked in with a healthy appetite. He was just about to go when Bartram said, 'Well, it's been fine for us having your company but you never told me your name.'

The traveller stood and looked long at the seated piper.

'My name is James – James Stewart – and I am your king,' he said, with a hard look.

'My – my lord,' Bartram stuttered as he fell on one knee, his wife making gasping noises in the corner. 'My lord . . . I am at your service.'

The king laughed. 'You certainly have been. I thank you for your kind hospitality. Now I must be on my way to Drumelzier.'

'Oh no, no, your majesty,' Bartram burst out. 'You will be in danger; Sir James's men will demand tribute from you and if you do not pay they are liable to attack you. You could even get killed if you don't let on who you are. He is a bully and a bandit, if you'll pardon me saying so, sire, and he has taken money from all of us poor people around here.'

'I thank you for warning me,' the king said. 'but I am in no danger. There's a troop of horse within earshot at all times and

137

all I have to do to summon them is blow this,' and he held up a silver whistle. 'I tell you what, though,' he went on, 'I am not too sure of the way to Drumelzier, so will you act as my guide?'

'It would be an honour, sire, a great honour,' replied the piper, still on one knee.

The king gently pulled him to his feet and, bidding farewell to his host's wife, the two set out on the road.

As they went, the king asked about Sir James and his bullying tactics in the area. Soon enough they were close to Drumelzier and there before them were two of Sir James's men, armed to the teeth, and behind them, sitting on his horse, was Sir James Tweedie.

'Right, you,' shouted one of the armed men, as they came close, 'doff your hats and get down on your knees. Have you no respect? This is Sir James Tweedie; show him some respect.'

As the two of them stood there, neither making any attempt to do as they were told, Tweedie himself shouted out, 'Right, teach these scum a lesson they won't forget, lads.'

The two men ran forward with their swords drawn. Bartram was knocked down by the flat of a sword. The other man, however, was a different matter entirely. As the bully looked on, getting angrier and angrier, the dusty traveller was easily keeping the two men at bay with skilful use of his staff. 'Get him,' cried Sir James, 'kill the beggar; he dares to stand against me.'

At that, the two men fell back to get a breath; the dusty traveller before them brought a whistle to his lips and gave three short blasts. The two soldiers looked at each other curiously. What was going on? As their master shouted at them to attack again, a drumming noise was heard. Then, around the bend in the road came a troop of mounted and armed men, all wearing the livery of the king. Within seconds, they had surrounded the two soldiers and Sir James Tweedie found himself looking at the point of a sword inches from his throat. Helping the piper to his feet, the king came forward towards Tweedie. The mounted men around the now frightened bully drew back as the king approached.

'Well, well, Sir James Tweedie,' he said in an authoritative voice, 'we have never met, but I am your king. Get down this instant.'

Tweedie threw himself from his horse and knelt on the ground before the king, spluttering and trying to apologise.

'Silence!' roared the king. 'You will appear before me at my palace two weeks from today and I shall deal with you then.' He turned to Bartram and smiled, 'And I would like to see you there too. One good turn deserves another.' And to Bartram's astonishment he winked at him.

Turning quickly, he leapt on Tweedie's horse and set off in the direction of Drumelzier at the head of his troops, leaving a bemused piper, two relieved soldiers and a frightened knight behind him. Tweedie knew that he had transgressed badly by having his men attack the king. The fact that the ruler was disguised as a poor man might even make matters worse, for Tweedie had heard the rumours that the king was concerned about the welfare of all his citizens. Over the next two weeks, he managed to convince himself that the king couldn't be mad enough to care about the poor, and he was sure that once he explained himself he would be forgiven, or at the worst, be made to pay a fine.

So the day came round when Bartram made his way to the king's palace. He was shown into a great room full of people dressed in finery and there at the end of the hall, and much more resplendent than any of his courtiers, was King James himself. As the piper watched, Sir James Tweedie was brought before his king. There, on his knees, he heard his fate. He was to lose all his lands and be sent into exile. If he ever showed his face in Scotland again his life would be forfeit. As the white-faced and shaking Tweedie was shown past him to the door, Bartram was called forward.

'Ah, my good friend Bartram,' the king smiled, 'I thank you for your hospitality. I enjoyed your company and also your piping. You are a good musician and, though a poor man, you made me as welcome as it was in your power to do. So that in future you will have a bit more time for your piping, I hereby grant you enough land to keep a mare and a foal, a pig and her litter and five pastures for sheep on Holms Common. Go off, and be well Bartram; your king thanks you and may God go with you.'

From then on, whenever there was company in Bartram's new house, and as a man who loved conviviality there were many such nights, he would play his pipes with gusto and then tell the assembled company how he, a humble piper and cobbler, had been blessed by the king himself.

The Gaberlunzie Man

In the old times in Scotland there used to be an official kind of beggar. Clad in blue cloaks, these men were allowed to travel the country asking for money and food. They were known as gaberlunzies and were officially sanctioned, each of them having a badge as well as his blue cloak to prove he had the right to beg in Scotland's villages and towns. The institution lasted for a long time in the late Middle Ages and the gaberlunzies were accepted as an everyday part of society. One time, in the Borders, a hairst (harvest) dance had been organised by a wealthy local farmer, Willie Hume of Cairnkebbie. Hairst dances were common throughout Scotland but Willie Hume's hairst dance was famous. He never stinted, always laying on lots of good food and drink for his farm workers and for the neighbours as well. Now, Willie was as proud as punch of his daughter Lily, a real bonny lass who had caught the eye of many a young lad in the area. However, she cared only for Will Kerr, a local shepherd with whom she had fallen in love. Will loved her more than life itself, but they both knew that her father would not sanction their marriage, as young Kerr had no money and Willie Hume wanted his treasured lass to marry well and have a good life. The young couple had resolved that they would do something to sort out their situation but had as yet not managed to figure anything out. The day of the dance came round and people began to make their way to Willie Hume's big barn, everybody dressed up in their very best and looking forward to having a grand old time. A local piper had been hired and the barn was all set up. Soon the music began and the drink began to flow as people started enjoying themselves.

The dance had only been going a short while when there was a knocking on the barn door. Willie Hume was sure that everyone he had invited was already there and went to the door, wondering who could be there.

He opened the door; there stood a tall and well-built man in the blue cloak of a gaberlunzie, with a bundle on his shoulder. In his old bonnet he had a peacock's feather and he wore a great smile.

'Would ye have room for another at the hairst dance, Mr Hume?' asked the smiling man.

Willie knew fine that he was well known in the area, so was in no way surprised that this strolling beggar knew who he was. He thought for a moment.

'All right, then,' he said. 'Come awa in and join the dance. It's open house anyway.'

So the gaberlunzie came in and, boy, did he show himself to be a jolly beggar. He danced with as many of the lassies as he could, stealing kisses from some of the young, and not so young, women, cracking jokes, telling stories and generally being the life and soul of the party. His dancing in particular was remarkable. He would leap high in the air with one arm up, the other hand resting on his hip and let out a mighty 'Hooch,' before landing lightly on his toes. He was making people laugh, both the women and the men. Then, as one dance finished, he dashed over to the bales of straw that the piper was standing on.

'Could I borrow yer pipes man, so I can play these grand people a tune or two?' he asked with a beaming smile. Now, the piper had noticed just what a live wire the gaberlunzie was and gladly handed over his pipes, reckoning that he would have a chance for a few drinks himself while the beggar played. So the gaberlunzie struck up a lively tune and the whole crowd got up on their feet to dance. The gaberlunzie played well indeed and the dance whirled round and round.

After a while he stopped to catch his breath, and was roundly applauded. There were even some cheers for him as the original piper came over, took back the pipes and started up again.

As he came off the straw bales the gaberlunzie found himself beside Lily. He noticed that she looked a little down and asked her what was wrong.

'Ach, it's nothing, never mind me,' she said.

'No, no, I can tell something isnae right, lassie. Sometimes it helps to tell a stranger yer troubles, ye ken,' he said with a sympathetic smile.

Lily looked at him and thought he looked like an under-standing soul. So she told him of her love for young Will Kerr and her father's opposition because of Will's lack of money. The gaberlunzie was sympathetic and told her not to lose hope; that things had a way of working themselves out and that maybe she and Will would have a life together. Now, Lily realised that this was just a beggar she was talking to, but something in his kindly smile and sympathetic manner made her feel that maybe he was right – maybe things could yet work out for her and Will.

There was a break in the dancing and people started to tell stories. After three of four weel-kennt stories had been told, the gaberlunzie man stepped up and asked if the company didn't mind him having a go at the storytelling. Now everyone there was already impressed by this fine-looking beggar and his suggestion met with approval; so he started and within minutes the whole place was heaving with laughter. Not only could he play the pipes; he was a grand storyteller as well. He was going down very well and even Willie Hume was heard to say, 'He's a fine fellow, him, a real turn, and he'll be welcome here anytime.' All around him agreed that this particular blue-cloak, as they were sometimes known, was a remarkable man indeed.

The dancing was just about to start when horses were heard approaching the barn. Suddenly, the barn door swung open and there in the doorway was a man dressed in the livery of the king's messenger. They might never have seen the king, but they all knew what his official representative in the area looked like. He drew his sword and half a dozen soldiers came in behind him. He looked around and then pointed to the straw bales the piper was standing on, interrupting him just as he was about to start playing again.

'Right, men,' he commanded, 'there it is!' and pointed with his sword at the bundle. At once two soldiers ran and brought the bundle back to him. Willie Hume stepped forward and was just about to ask what they thought they were doing when the messenger put away his sword and grabbed the bundle from the soldier carrying it. Then he spoke again: 'In the king's name, pay attention. You have a thief here among you. Look.'

He unwrapped the bundle the gaberlunzie had been carrying, and there was a beautiful silver mace.

'This man here, this gaberlunzie, stole this mace from a procession on the streets of Dundee and we have come to take him before the king for trial and execution.'

At that, the gaberlunzie moved like lightning, grabbing the mace and running to stand on the straw bales beside the piper.

'I am Wat Wilson, the King of the Beggars, and I say I have the right to a mace of my own,' he shouted, waving it above his head. 'Come and get it if you can.'

The soldiers at once headed towards him but suddenly found their way blocked. Willie Hume spoke: 'This man is a guest of ours. How dare you come bursting in here with drawn swords, frightening the womenfolk.'

The women around the place all looked at each other. Them frightened! Not hardly.

'Out of my way, farmer,' shouted the king's messenger, grabbing Hume by the arm as if to throw him bodily aside. At that, no doubt a bit fired up by drink, but also feeling a bit of sympathy for the charming gaberlunzie, Will Kerr and a few more of the young men stepped forward and threw the king's messenger off Hume. Then all hell let loose. Soldiers and farm workers were fighting all over the barn. The soldiers had little chance, however. They were outnumbered about eight to one; in a few minutes they found themselves locked inside the barn, while the rest of the company were outside laughing and joking and having a drink or two more. The gaberlunzie borrowed the pipes again and marched around the barn, playing a triumphal march to general applause and laughter. The he ran to the barn door and shouted through it, 'When I next see the king I'll tell him you tried your best.'

This too was met with hoots of laughter. The gaberlunzie then went and thanked Willie Hume for his hospitality and his help. He then took the messenger's horse and rode away, waving the great silver mace above his head.

A short while later in Willie Hume's kitchen there was a sad scene. His wife was sitting sobbing her heart out.

'Willie Hume, you great fool,' she panted between sobs. 'Fighting with the king's men. They'll hang you for this, mark my words, and the king will likely take the land. What will me and Lily do then? Oh, Willie, you great fool.'

'Well, that gaberlunzie was a fine lad, and they should no have come into the barn like that, wi drawn swords and frightenin folk,' he replied in a downcast voice. The effects of the whisky had worn off a bit and he was just about beginning to appreciate the trouble he could be in. Will Kerr was there, standing with Lily in the corner, wondering what was going to happen and how it might affect them, when the kitchen door swing open.

It was the king's messenger, who had eventually managed to break free from the barn.

'Willie Hume,' he said in an ominous voice, 'I instruct ye in the name o yer king tae be at the Great Hall in Holyrood Palace a week from today, to answer for your deeds this day.'

He glared at the farmer, who gulped and nodded.

'I'll come along wi you,' said Will Kerr. 'It was me that started the whole thing and I'll tell the king that.'

'Ach, thanks, laddie,' said Hume. 'Ye're a good lad, right enough, just as Lily says. But it was my barn, my dance and it all happened on my land. It's me that must tak whatever's comin.'

It was a sad night at Cairnkebbie that night, as they all thought of the fate that could be awaiting the farmer. Laying hands on the king's messenger in the pursuance of his duty was no simple act. The penalty would likely be hanging, and maybe confiscation of all his lands and goods as well. His wife and daughter could easily end up penniless.

A week later Willie Hume and Will Kerr were in Edinburgh. They made their way to the palace and were eventually shown into the great hall. There sat the king, resplendent in crown and robes, surrounded by gaudily dressed courtiers and a troop of soldiers. The messenger was standing close by.

The king's messenger called Hume's name and he stepped forward. Will Kerr made to join him but was pushed back by a couple of soldiers.

'Of what is this man charged?' asked the king.

'He fought with your messenger in defence of a known thief,' replied the man.

'Is this true?' asked the king of Hume, who was kneeling before him with his head bent.

'Aye, your Majesty. I cannae deny it. I did fight wi your messenger to defend thon man.'

'And why did you do such a thing?' the king asked.

Willie took a deep breath and said, 'Well, ye see, Your Majesty,

145

thon gaberlunzie fellow your men were chasin was a fine man. He had been entertainin everybody at the hairst dance: he was funny, he could dance like a grasshopper and he was a braw, braw piper as well. We aye have a good time at the dancin but he just made everybody feel happier. He told us some rare stories as well. He was right jolly fellow and we just thought we should come to his aid, that's all.'

All of this was said with his head down.

'Well, then,' said the king, 'how about telling me one of these supposedly funny stories?'

Willie looked up briefly, but such was his sense of resignation to his fate he hardly registered the look on the king's face. He didn't even notice that the king was smiling slightly. So Willie told one of the gaberlunzie's stories and the entire room burst into laughter, particularly the king.

Willie just knelt there, totally bemused by what was going on. What was happening? Why was the king laughing? Was he going to be executed or not?

The king stood up, put his hand on the shoulder of the kneeling farmer and turned to his messenger.

'Right. I told you I could raise my own people against you, Thomas. You had better pay up the debt,' he said with a smile.

'I accept, sire, you win. You were right,' replied the messenger, who was also grinning broadly.

Now, Willie Hume hadn't cottoned on yet. He was so busy worrying about what was about to happen that he couldn't concentrate on what was being said.

'Willie Hume,' said the king.

'Yes, sire,' he replied in a trembling voice.

'Do you know the penalty for interfering with the king's messenger on his lawful business?' he demanded.

'Aye, sire.' He paused. 'The penalty is death.'

There was a complete silence in the great hall as the king spoke again.

'Well, just wait till I put on my hat and I will give you your sentence.'

A courtier handed the king a battered old hat with a peacock feather on it, which he put on his head, as another courtier handed him the royal mace.

'Now, Willie Kerr,' the king said, 'look at me.'

Slowly, keeping as tight a grip as he could on his emotions, Willie Kerr raised his head. He looked up and there was the gaberlunzie man!

As he fell over in astonishment, the whole court erupted in laughter and the king's messenger helped Willie to his feet. He stood there, mouth hanging open, looking at his king. The gaberlunzie man.

'Well, do you think I made a jolly beggar then, Willie?' he asked, laughing.

All Willie could do was stammer assent. He was overwhelmed. He wasn't going to die.

Then the king held up his hand. The room fell silent again.

'Right, then. Willie Hume, I am commanding you to give your agreement to the marriage of your Lily to Will Kerr. I will grant him lands enough that your daughter will want for nothing. Will you do this?'

Hume looked at his king and nodded.

'Good. Now you must tell no one what has passed here this day. I want you to keep it to yourself, but for your assistance in helping the gaberlunzie man.' And, at that, he smiled again. 'From this time on you own Cairnkebbie forever. It is your freehold. Do just try and look after the odd beggar as they pass.'

When Hume and Kerr got back to Cairnkebbie together they were welcomed by two tearful women, who had never expected to see them again. When they heard what the king had done and who he was Lily was beside herself with joy, and only a few weeks later she was married to Will Kerr. It was a grand wedding and, as usual, Willie Hume wasn't afraid of putting his hand in his pocket. But, people agreed, it wasn't as much fun as the time the gaberlunzie man came to Willie Hume's hairst dance and played the pipes.

Lowland Pipers

Throughout the Middle Ages bagpipes were common in the Lowlands of Scotland, and the institution of town pipers was widespread. Though their functions were different from those of pipers in the Highlands, both had an important, even central, social role in their communities. Probably the best known of the Lowland pipers was Habbie Simpson, whose story is the first one told here. His memory survives because of an elegy to him by the poet Robert Semple, rather than because of his piping skills. We do know that amongst his repertoire were tunes that had been mentioned as early as the fifteenth century. The last remnants of the institution of town pipers disappeared from the Lowlands, along with all sorts of patronage, after the Reform Act of 1833, just at the time when the 'Highland' bagpipe was coming to the fore in popularity through the annual competitions of the Highland societies.

Habbie Simpson

Habbie Simpson was the town piper of Kilbarchan in Renfrewshire in the early seventeenth century. His position was apparently his alone, there not having been one before or after him, and he is said to have been the butt of many a practical joke in his time. It seems unlikely that he had a piper's croft, though he probably did receive some sort of salary for his performances. It is said that his tombstone referred to him as combining the role of town piper with that of a butcher, and it is believed that amongst his repertoire were tunes that had been mentioned as early as the fifteenth century. He seems to have played at all the festivities that happened in his time in Kilbarchan.

Habbie, however, has another reputation. The local laird was called Johnstone and one day the laird's wife was told that Habbie's wife had come to call at the big house. She was ushered in and appeared to be in a terrible state.

'Mrs Simpson, is something wrong?' enquired Mrs Johnstone.

'Och, ma'am, it's Habbie, ma poor Habbie, he's deid an has left me without a penny piece. I dinna ken what I'll dae; I've nae money tae bury the poor auld man.' And, saying this, she burst into tears.

Mrs Johnstone might have been a lady, but she was human and her sympathy was touched. So she gave Mrs Simpson several pounds to help her in her troubles, and in those days that was a lot of money.

Unknown to Mrs Johnstone, that same day her husband was in a tavern in the town sealing some business over a glass of claret, when he was approached by the poor dead Habbie himself. The piper was red-eyed and clearly distraught.

'Good day, Simpson,' said the laird. 'Are you all right, man?'

'Och, good day tae ye, sir. I'm afraid I'm no verra weel at all. Ma poor wife has just died and I hae nae money tae bury the poor thing.' At which he burst into tears.

Like his wife, Johnstone was a sympathetic human being and decided to help the distraught piper in his troubles. So he too reached into his pocket and handed over several pounds.

How the pair of them thought they could get away with such a ploy in a small place like Kilbarchan beggars belief. Later that same night they were celebrating their success in one of the coarser hostelries of the area in company with a few friends, of the sort who always appear when money and drink are flowing freely, when who should appear but Mr Johnstone himself. He had been tipped off to the trick by one of his servants and we can imagines the blustering performance that Habbie put on to try and justify himself.

It was probably from this time on that Habbie became the butt of humour, which in time led to his being immortalised in the truly pathetic work by Semple. The picture Semple paints is of someone who was of some importance to the community. The poem delineates some of the functions that a town piper was expected to fulfil, such as playing at public events, leading the bride to church and playing at the Wappinshaw, when the men of the neighbourhood were obliged to turn out with their weaponry to show their fitness for battle, if it should be required. Apart from the almost constant threat of possible invasion from Scotland's southron neighbours, the raiding activities of Border families, like those of the Highland clans, made it a necessary aspect of Scottish society to be on one's guard.

The Epitaph of Habbie Simpson, Piper of Kilbarchan

Kilbarchan now may say alas!
For she has lost her game and grace,
Both Trixie and the Maiden Tree:
But what remeed?
For no man can supply his place:
Hab Simson's dead.

Now who shall play The Day it Dawis,
Or Hunt's Up, when the cock he craws?
Or who can for our kirk-town cause
Stand us in stead?
On bagpipes now nobody blaws
Sen Habbie's dead.

Or who will cause our shearers shear?
Wha will bend up the brags o weir,
Bring in the bells, or good play-meir

In time of need?
Hab Simpson could, what needs you speir,
But now he's dead.

So kindly to his neighbours neist
At Beltane and St Berchan's feast
He blew, and then held I up his breast,
As he were weid:
But now we need not him arrest,
For Habbie's dead.

At fairs he play'd before the spear-men,
All gaily graithed in their gear, man:
Steel bonnets, jacks and swords so clear then
Like ony bead:
Now wha will play before such weir-men
Sen Habbie's dead.

At clerk-plays when he wont to come.
His pipe played trimly to the drum;
Like bikes of bees he gart it hum.
And tun'd his reed:
Now all our pipers may sing dumb,
Sen Habbie's dead.

And at horse races many a day,
Before the black, the brown, the grey,
He gart his pipe, when he did play,
Baith skirl and skreed:
Now all such pastime's quite away
Sen Habbie's dead.

He counted was a waled wight-man,
And fiercely at football he ran:

At every game the gree he wan
For pith and speed.
The like of Habbie wasna then
Bit now he's dead.

And then, besides his valiant acts,
At bridals he wan many placks;
He bobbit ay behind folk's backs
And shook his head.
Now we want many merry cracks
Sen Habbie's dead.

He was convoyer of the bride,
With Kittoch hanging at his side;
About the kirk he thought a pride
The ring to lead:
But now we may gae but a guide,
For Habbie's dead.

So well's he kept his decorum,
And all the stots of Whip-meg-morum:
He slew a man, and wae's me for him
And bure the feid!
But yet the man wan hame before him,
And was not dead.

And when he play'd, the lasses leugh
To see him toothless, auld and teugh.
He was his pipes besides Barcleugh,
Withouten dread!
Which after wan him gear enough;
But now he's dead.

Ay when he play'd the gaislings gedder'd,

And when he spake the carl bledder'd
On Sabbath days his cap was fedder'd,
A seemly weid;
In the kirk-yeard his mare stood tedder'd,
Where he lies dead.

Alas! for him my heart is sair,
For of his spring I gat a skair,
At every play, race, feast, or fair,
But guile or dread;
We need not look for piping mair,
Sen Habbie's dead.

Sir Robert Semple of Beltrees

The Sanquhar Piper

Although nowadays people tend to think of the bagpipes as a purely Highland instrument, the true story is that the pipes were played all over Scotland, just as different types of bagpipe are still played all over Europe and indeed the world. At one point the bagpipes were even common in England! Many a Lowland town had its town piper, who in some ways was a bit like the clan piper of the Highlands. He had certain duties and responsibilities and, though he might not be called to lead the fighting men of the clan into battle, the town piper was man of some standing in the local community. There are no recorded Lowland master pipers or supposed schools of piping like the one at Boreraig in Skye; though there were regular duties, such as playing at certain times of the day and on particular occasions, the Lowland pipers never seem to have had quite the role of the clan pipers. Their cultural importance, however, was significant.

In Sanquhar, in Dumfriesshire, they long had a town piper, one of whose daily duties was to march through the town from the

Gallows Knowe near the old castle, through the town square to
the piper's thorn. This daily march was a regular, colourful and
well-liked event in town life and people would stop in the street
to watch the piper pass. Children would often follow him too,
and it is not unlikely that now and again a few of them would be
taking the mick – such are bairns.

Underneath the piper's thorn, a stone seat had been set up and
here the piper would sit after his perambulation and maybe have
a wee sup of something to keep the cold out and tiredness away.
Back in the seventeenth century, pipers were as well known for
their drouth, or thirst, as they have been ever since. But back
then times were often terrible. In the 1640s the country was
racked with civil war between the forces of the king and the
Covenanters, who resisted the erosion of what they considered
their religious liberties. Things had got steadily worse and many
a man, woman and child fell in this struggle between two different aspects of the same religion. The king wanted to impose
bishops on the people and many tens of thousands of the people
of Scotland had set their faces against that. They had drawn up
the Solemn League and Covenant in 1638 and swore to uphold
the Presbyterian religion. No matter where you were in Scotland
at the time it was difficult to escape the religious wars and bigo-
try, and Sanquhar was no exception. The Southern Uplands were
a favourite spot for conventicles (illegal outdoor prayer meetings
held by the Presbyterian Covenanters). Up there on the moors
many of them felt even closer to God, and they had far less
chance of being attacked by government troops outside the
towns.

The government, however, had troops roaming the Southern
Uplands on the look-out for the rebel Covenanters. The
Sanquhar town piper was a convivial and friendly soul who had
no great love of religion. He just wanted a quiet life, the chance
to play his pipes and have the necessary for the odd sip or two of
the whisky. Given his habit of indulging himself in a wee drink,

he had been warned by his friends to take care if there were any government troops about. Many of the soldiers thought that the entire population were rebels and tended to shoot first and ask questions later, if at all. One afternoon, after having done the piper's walk in the town that morning, the piper was visiting a friend who lived out on the moors above Sanquhar. As the day wore on, they found themselves getting 'fou', as the bard says, and by nightfall the piper was pretty drunk. On his way back he tripped and fell in a ditch up by the Black Loch and, finding himself stuck, simply went to sleep. He had missed the evening perambulation which was part of his job, but it wasn't the first time that had happened. It was to be the last.

He awoke, early on a grey and misty morning, shivering a bit with the cold. He knew he would feel a lot better once he got back to the town and had a hot meal. So he dragged himself to his feet from the hollow where he had fallen and set off across the moors towards Sanquhar.

Unknown to the piper, however, a troop of government soldiers was on the moor. They were looking for a fugitive Covenanter that one of their spies had told them was hiding out on the moor. They had been up since dawn, making a sweep across the moor. Suddenly one of the soldiers saw a figure through the mist.

'Over here, lads,' he shouted, then called through the swirling mist, 'Stop in the king's name!'

All the piper heard was a vague shout somewhere behind him and, in his eagerness to get home and do something about his hangover, he ignored it. This was a fatal mistake. The soldier drew aim on the figure ahead of him. As the morning mist swirled away, other soldiers had a clear view of the piper. They were in no doubt that this was the fugitive who had dragged them out on this cold and nasty morning on this Scottish moor. A volley of shots rang out and the piper fell – dead. When the soldiers came up to him, their officer realised that this was not their intended prey, but the Sanquhar piper. He and his troops had been briefly billeted in the town the previous week. However, the fool had refused to stop when commanded so, as far as he was concerned, his men had had every right to shoot him.

The officer at least had the decency to send the body back to Sanquhar, carried by his men, all of whom regretted the incident but saw it as just one of those things. Back up on the moors, the officer, maybe feeling a wee bit guilty, had his men raise a cairn where the piper fell, and it has been known ever since as the Piper's Cairn.

The house where the piper lived at Closeburn in Sanquhar later changed its name. In their wisdom, and not at all influenced by prevailing fashion, the town council decided to have a town fiddler rather than a town piper. One of the incumbents of that position was a noted fiddler, James Kerr, and from his time on the house was known as the Fiddler's Close.

Sanquhar's Last Piper

The last town piper of Sanquhar was Sandy Holton, a canny, happy-go-lucky sort of a man. He was a fine piper and well liked about the town, probably because he was such a convivial soul; he liked nothing better than sitting with friends, having a crack and swapping stories. There was one blight on his life, though. His wife, Jeanie, was a right shrew of a woman. Nothing he ever did pleased her: he never made enough money; he was too often out with his friends and he didn't pay her enough attention. She was one of those people for whom the glass is always half empty, never half full. If there was reason to moan, she'd find it; if there wasn't, she'd make one up. With this irascible nature there went a biting tongue. She knew how to hurt people, especially Sandy, and, although he was a sociable soul, his friends all avoided going to his home. Jeanie realised this was her fault, but it just made her even more ill-tempered. Sandy, playing at weddings and dances, was very popular – 'The lasses danced as they were mad/ When he blew the chanter' – and occasionally one or two of the lassies made eyes at Sandy. But he never responded, though Jeanie accused him of it often enough. Despite her nagging and shrewish ways, Sandy stuck it out with her; he was an honest man and had taken her for better or for worse.

'If I'd kennt at the time whit I ken nou, though, things micht hae been different,' he was heard to say on more than one occasion to his friends. Still, he struggled on, year after year. They were never blessed with children and Sandy knew deep in his heart that this was probably the reason Jeanie was such an unhappy creature. He too would have liked to have had bairns, but such was his nature that he never dwelt on the past or on life's disappointments. He felt quite sorry for Jeanie, when she wasn't nagging him about one thing or another.

After many rather unhappy years together, Jeanie suddenly took ill and died. It happened in less than a week. People came round to express their condolences to Sandy but, in the nature of things, after a commiserating drink or two, the condolences turned into congratulations. Everybody thought he was much better off without Jeanie. Now, funerals in those days, as with some today, were often the occasion for a great deal of serious drinking. It was one way of dealing with sorrow; but funerals are also essentially social occasions, where people who don't see each other that often meet up. This in itself was often the starting point for a considerable drinking session, but with Jeanie's death the whole town of Sanquhar thought that Sandy's life would be much improved. And that was certainly a good excuse for a celebration.

Accordingly, the night before the funeral, a great deal of drink had been brought into Sandy's house for the 'kistin'. This was the name given to the eve of the funeral, when the body was laid out in the coffin on a table in the best room in the house. A plate of salt was placed on the breast of the corpse to keep away evil spirits and sometimes pennies were placed on the eyes to ensure that the lids stayed shut. Various superstitious traditions took place: all the milk in the house was thrown out and all perishable goods had a nail or piece of wire stuck in them. This, it was believed, stopped food and drink from going off and was, of course, particularly important when it came to whisky. Candlesticks were usually placed at the head of the coffin to shed light on the face of the departed. As only men attended funerals in most parts of Scotland till very recently, the kistin gave the womenfolk a chance to say farewell. Though in Jeanie's case most people were glad to see the back of her.

So glad, in fact, that at the kistin, after a few bottles had been passed around the gathered crew, things were quite jolly. Because of Sandy's popularity as a piper, a lot of the younger lads and lasses of the town who regularly attended every dance and social occasion in the area knew him well and turned up.

'Ach, weel,' said the souter, Thomas Bodkin, 'ye'll have an easier road tae run now, Sandy.'

This was met with muttered sounds of agreement from the company. Then the local blacksmith James Fenton spoke up: 'Ay, ay, Sandy, ye'll have some peace at last.'

One or two of the women tried to shush the men, but half-heartedly; Jeanie really had offended the whole town at one time or another. The few relations she had in Thornhill, twelve miles to the south, were expected to turn up at the funeral briefly, if at all.

The bottle passed round again and again, and it wasn't long till one of the younger lasses was on her feet and looking to dance.

'Come on, Sandy, gie us a blaw,' said her companion. The rest of the company looked at one another, then at Sandy, who was sitting, looking a bit quizzical.

'Och, why not,' he said, and went to pull out a set of bellows pipes from below the bed. Out came the wee pipes and, within minutes, a lively dance was taking place around the coffin, with poor Jeanie lying there.

Fenton leaned over the coffin at one point and said, 'Well then, Jeanie, there's a ceilidh in your house after aw, here's tae ye,' and drank off a large glass of straight whisky.

The dancers danced, the piper piped and the bottle whirled round and round.

Before they knew it, they had danced the night away and dawn was streaking the sky. Realising that Jeanie's grave was already dug, Sandy had what he thought was a grand idea.

'Right,' he shouted, putting down the wee pipes, 'let's just get Jeanie tae the kirkyard nou. The grave is ready dug and ye ken whit they say – there's nae time like the present.'

Being as fou as the piper, the rest of the company agreed. So, after nailing down the coffin lid, Sandy lifted up his bagpipes and organised half a dozen of the younger lads to hoist the coffin on their shoulders. Then they all headed off to the churchyard.

The people of Sanquhar were roused from their beds just after dawn by the sound of the pipes playing a merry reel. When they looked out of their windows they saw the town piper striding along, blowing up a storm, followed by his wife's coffin on the shoulders of half a dozen local lads, and behind them a crowd of clearly merry revellers. This was a sight indeed and many came to their doors to watch the strange procession. A few followed on at the tail of the funeral party.

On getting to the kirkyard, the lads took the coffin to the newly-dug grave and lowered it in. Then they filled in the grave and all the time Sandy played away grand style. Given the circumstances, it is little wonder that the party, plus a few more, headed back to Sandy's house at Closeburn to continue the festivities. They carried on till they dropped! Others arrived in the course of the day and, after a few hours' sleep, Sandy awoke to find his house still full of revellers and picked up his pipes again. The party lasted three full days as people came to give their condolences! Sandy's popularity ensured there was a steady stream of visitors over those days, many of them carrying their own bottles. The party was talked about for years.

As for Sandy, despite the encouragement of his friends, he never married again.

'Tae be bitten aince is experience; twice would be just daft,' he used to say when pushed on the subject. Truth to tell, he always remembered what Jeanie had been like when he married her and never lost all his feelings for her.

So he lived on to a good old age, giving pleasure to the community with his piping and cheery attitude.

One time, after a local barn dance he was asleep in his bed when a wild storm blew up and took away the thatch on his cottage. When his friends came round to see how he was, he simply said, 'Ach weel, if the win has blawn aff the roof, the win'll jist hae tae blaw it back again,' turned over and went back to sleep. He meant, that playing his pipes, he would soon bring in sufficient funds to pay for a new roof. And he did.

The Wandering Piper

This story took place a while ago now. There was this man used to wander the whole of Scotland. He was a piper and a bit of a handyman. He could turn his hand to most kinds of jobs and, in those days, a man who could do joinery work, fencing, roofing and basic iron work was generally welcome at farmhouses and out-of-the-way villages. He could pick up work at the many farms and wee villages scattered around the countryside and play his pipes in the bigger villages and towns. It was a way of life that he enjoyed, though it wasn't always an easy type of existence. Winters especially could be really hard but he was strong and healthy and, having slept below the stars for most of his life, he didn't tend to worry too much about finding a place to sleep of a night. He was happy wandering from place to place with just the clothes he wore, his pipes and his bag of tools.

However, he tended to try and get himself some place to stay over the worst months of the winter, and particularly liked to make sure he had somewhere to celebrate Hogmanay with a good crowd.

This year things hadn't worked out to his satisfaction and he found himself on the road at Hogmanay. The weather had been particularly nasty since Christmas and now, on the last night of the year, a real blizzard was blowing up. The piper had intended heading for a farm where he knew he would be made welcome to play in the New Year, but somehow, despite his knowledge and sense of direction, he found himself off his road. Somewhere or another he had made a wrong turning. It was well after dark; the snow was coming at him in vicious gusts; the temperature seemed to be dropping even further and he was beginning to get a bit desperate. His old boots were splitting along the seams and his feet were beginning to go numb – something he knew was dangerous. He was wrapped up in an old greatcoat, a scarf across his face, and a bonnet jammed down over his ears. As he struggled against the wind he suddenly stumbled and fell. Something was in the middle of the road.

Picking himself up, he kicked at the lump in the snow. It felt hard and, whatever it was, it was a goodly size – there was a hump in the snow nearly six feet long. He knelt down and scraped away the snow. 'Great heavens,' he thought, 'it's a man.' Just then the snow died away and he looked up into a clear sky. His first thought was to get the man upright, but he noticed that the man was well and truly dead. In fact he was frozen solid there in the middle of a deserted back country road. He must have been there for several days; he was like a block of ice. Looking down at the man, once he had cleared the snow off him, he noticed that he was wearing what seemed to be a new pair of boots. Now, they might not have been brand new but, compared to the flapping pair that were on the piper's feet, they were as good as. What is more, they seemed to be the same size as his own!

'Well, ma freend, ye've nae use for these boots now and my feet are fair freezin. These boots of yours would do me just brawly, an I'm pretty shair ye'll no mind.'

So he tried to untie the laces of the man's boots, but of course they were frozen solid. He tried chipping away at them with the chisel from his tool bag, but without any success. So he squatted by the side of the corpse and thought about things. His own boots were well past it and if he continued wearing them in this weather he knew he was risking frostbite. But how could he get the boots of the dead man? Then he had it. He reached into his tool bag and pulled out a tenon saw. He would saw off both feet and wait for an opportunity to thaw the boots off them! So that's what he did and, just as he got the second foot – and boot – off, the sky clouded over and the snow came on again. Taking a piece of strong twine from his bag, he tied the feet together and hung them round his neck. He knew that he hadn't passed any houses or farms for miles, so he had no choice but to go on.

An hour or so later, through the blowing snow, he caught sight of a light. Thank heavens, he thought, a house, and headed straight for it. The snow soon blanked out the light but he kept on, crossing dykes and fences, till at last the snow again briefly cleared and he saw a small farm about a quarter of a mile away. So on he plodded, getting more tired by the second. He was fit and strong but this weather was draining him of all his energy and he couldn't feel his own feet at all. At last he came up to the farm. Light was streaming out of the window and he looked in. There was an old couple sitting by a roaring fire. Between them was a table and on that table was a sight that made him feel faint. A freshly-cooked chicken was steaming on a plate surrounded with vegetables, and next to it was a full bottle of whisky. All at once he felt the juices in his mouth begin to run. This was Hogmanay night and the couple were going to see in the New Year with a feast and a good drink. Surely they would offer him hospitality on this night of the year. Giving himself a shake, he knocked on the door. There was no answer, so he knocked again.

Eventually, he heard someone coming to the door.

'Who's there?' came the old man's voice.

'I'm a travellin piper, caught out in the storm and looking for a bit of shelter and heat. A Happy Hogmanay to you,' he replied, through teeth that were beginning to chatter.

'Away with you,' came the reply. 'This is a respectable house; we have nothing to do with tramps and other wastrels here.'

'Man, I'm freezin to death out here,' the piper said, shocked by the man's indifference to his plight.

'That's none of my business,' the man said back. 'There's a village just five miles down the road. Why don't you go there?'

In the background the piper could hear the old woman whispering to the old man.

'We don't welcome tramps around here. Go on to the village,' the man repeated.

Standing there in the freezing cold, the piper heard the inner door of the house shut as the couple went back to the warm blazing fire in their front room. The snow was falling thicker and the wind was biting through his clothes. He knew if he tried to go another mile, never mind five, he might well freeze to death, just as the other fellow had. So he knocked again, as loud as he could.

'What do you want now?' the voice came again.

'For pity's sake, man. I just need some place to shelter from this storm; it's deathly cauld oot here.'

There was no immediate reply, but he could hear animated whispering.

'Well, alright then,' the man's voice came again, 'we'll have none of your kind in our house, but if you go round the back there's a byre and you can sleep in the straw with the cow. Good night.'

'Thank you,' said the piper through gritted teeth and went round the back of the farmhouse. Sure enough, there was a byre.

He pulled the door open, lit a match and saw there were two straw-filled stalls just inside the byre door. In one was a big old cow lying on her side, her head in a wooden rack of straw which she was calmly munching, the steam from her breath rising in a great cloud over her head. She looked at the piper, then ignored him. He moved into the other stall and made himself a space to sleep. Putting down his pipes, his tool bag and the two feet to one side, he snuggled down into the straw to sleep. It may not have been a feather bed in a mansion but he knew he would be fine now. The straw would keep him warm and his feet would soon get their feeling back.

He thought he should do something about them though. He sat up, took off his boots and began to rub his feet as hard as he could with his tough, calloused hands. Sitting doing this, a thought struck him. The thought made him chuckle. Standing up, he felt for the dead man's feet in the dark and picked them up. Simply by listening to the cow's breathing he made his way round into the other stall in the pitch black and felt his way along the cow's body. She hardly flinched. Finding the cow's head, he placed the tied together feet in the hay rack directly below the cow's nostrils. That should do it! With a bit of luck, once the morning came the feet would be warm enough to come out of the boots. Congratulating himself on his ingenuity, he snuggled down again into the straw and, exhausted as he was, soon fell sound asleep.

New Year's Day morning found him being wakened by the farm cockerel just as dawn was lightening the sky. He felt rested, but had a deep gnawing hunger in his belly. A dim light began to come in through the cracks in the byre walls – clearly it had stopped snowing. Standing up and stretching, he then went into the next stall to see what the boots were like. His trick had worked. The ice had melted and it took only a matter of minutes to extract the feet from the boots. He then tried on the boots and they were all warm from the cow's breath. They were a pretty fair fit. 'Lovely,' he thought. 'Just the very thing. That's a lot better.' He knew his toughened feet would soon help him break in these boots. He was pretty sure that the dead man on the road would not grudge him this. He was picking up his pipes and tool bag, intending to leave his old boots and the defrosted feet just where they were, when a thought struck him.

It would not have cost the old couple in the farm much to have invited him in to join them in a New Year's toast. In fact, not to have invited him in was extremely inhospitable; he had never heard of anything quite like it. Not to invite a stranger in on a deadly cold night was bad enough, but on the last night of the Old Year? That was disgraceful. Something should be done about such behaviour. He had to stop himself laughing out loud. He realised that one or other of the pair would soon be in to milk the cow and he did not want to have to come face to face with either of them. He would likely say something about their inhumane behaviour. So he carefully took the feet, placed them in his old boots, and put them in the hay rack. He then hid in a corner of the byre to await developments. Sure enough, a short time later the auld wife came in with a bucket in her hand, leaving the barn door open behind her. In the half-light of New Year's morning he watched as she poked the cow with a stick and pulled over a three-legged stool. The cow rose; the woman was just about to sit down and start milking the beast when she saw something. There in the hay rack at the head of the stall was a pair of feet in old battered and split boots.

She let out a terrible shriek and fell off the stool, kicking over the bucket and startling the cow, who began to kick up a fearsome noise. The old man came out to see what the fuss was about, but his wife lay there speechless, mouth hanging open, and pointed towards the hay rack.

'What?' the old man asked waspishly, 'what are you doing, what in God's name . . .'

He too was struck speechless when he saw the two booted feet nestling in the hay, just where the cow usually rested her head.

'Oh, my God,' he said. 'Oh, my God, Morag has eaten the tramp. All that's left are his boots. Oh, heavens, what will we do?'

'It's our cow that's killed him,' whispered his wife. 'What if anybody finds out?'

'Och, I'm sure they would put us in jail for this. They'll maybe transport us. Send us to the other side of the world,' said the farmer, now trembling with fear. 'We'll have to do something . . .'

'Aye, we will,' replied his wife, regaining some sort of control. 'But what?'

'We'll have to bury them and tell nobody. Ever. All right?' said the farmer, looking straight at his wife.

'Right,' she said, sounding relieved. 'But where can we bury them? The ground is frozen solid.'

'Aye, ye're right,' her husband replied, scratching his stubbly chin. 'The ground is a wee bit softer under the big cherry tree at the foot of the garden there. With a pick I'm sure I could dig there. I'll get the pick and a shovel and you, you bring the feet . . .'

All this while the piper was hiding, watching them. Not one word of sorrow, regret or sympathy had come from either of them. He was furious! All they were concerned with was their own safety. They had no human kindness in them at all. No wonder they hadn't invited him in to share their bottle of cratur! This pair needed seeing to, no doubt about it at all.

As the husband went to get his tools, the auld wife gingerly approached the hay rack. Screwing up her face and half looking away, she picked up the two feet, one in each hand, and went outside, leaving the door wide open. Carefully, the piper followed her, carrying his pipes and tool bag. Peeping round the byre door, he saw the coast was clear and went to the corner of the farmhouse. Again peering carefully round the edge of the house, he saw the old couple heading toward the foot of the garden, the man carrying a pick and shovel and his wife holding the feet at arm's length. They got to underneath the cherry tree and the man set to with the pick.

There were curses and shouts; the ground proved to be pretty resistant but, after a few minutes, driven by fear of discovery, he had managed to break the surface of the frozen earth and was busy digging a deep hole with the shovel. All the time the piper watched them.

The woman put the feet in the old twisted boots into the hole and the farmer proceeded to fill up the hole again.

Then, after stamping on the ground and brushing snow over the spot, the farmer picked up his pick and shovel and the pair of them headed back to the farmhouse and warmth of the fire. As he watched them go, the piper knew what he had to do. They headed back inside to get a hot cup of tea and probably a stiff drink of whisky; the piper went around behind the house and into the field, where he crouched down and made his way down to the bottom of the garden. He climbed the dyke and stood just behind the big tree. The weak midwinter sun had broken through and there, directly over where they had buried the feet, his shadow was falling. Taking his pipes from their box, he slowly blew in till the bag was full. Then he launched into an ancient and wild-sounding pibroch!

Up at the farmhouse, the couple were just about to drink their tea when they heard a noise like a banshee wailing from the bottom of their garden.

Scattering cups and teapot, they ran to the window and looked toward the cherry tree.

'Oh, my God, what's happening?' demanded the auld wife in a querulous voice.

'I'm no sure but . . . Oh, God save us, look, look,' gasped the farmer.

'What can you see?' his wife demanded, panic rising in her voice.

'Look. It's the piper. It's his ghost. He's come back to haunt us . . .' the man stammered.

'I said you should've let him in last night,' his wife screamed.

'No ye didnae, no ye didnae,' stammered the man. 'He's come back to haunt us. He must be after revenge for us letting him die oot there in the byre. We'll never be free o him. What if he comes up to the hoose? Come on, let's get out o here. Run, run for your life,' he shouted, heading for the door.

Stopping only to grab her bag and the tin where she had her savings, the auld wife followed the farmer out of the door and off they scuttled as fast as they could towards the village.

Once they were gone, the piper stopped playing and began to laugh as he walked to the farmhouse. There he put more coals on the fire, helped himself to the whisky left in the bottle and ate the remains of the chicken still sitting on the table from the night before. He had a fine day as he sat there finishing off the whisky and thinking to himself: 'Well, that'll maybe teach them a lesson about no treatin people with a bit of decency. They'll maybe remember tae be hospitable in the future.'

So he spent a warm and cosy night in the farmhouse. He could be there yet, as it's a known fact that the farmer and his wife never dared to go back and face the Ghost of the Piper's Feet.

A Piper of Renown

The last official town-crier of Kirkwall in Orkney was a real Scottish 'lad o pairts'. Apart from his job as town-crier, Jamie Wallace was a fine piper and made use of his musical talents in his official position. He was wont to rouse the workers from their beds, playing a tune on the pipes as he marched down the main street. Every day except Sunday he would start at the top end of the High Street and make his way down to the quay at the harbour, making sure everyone could hear him as he passed. His lung power was prodigious, a blessing for both the official crying of town news and piping. One of his other duties was to ring the town bell at eight o'clock in the evening. It was an unaccustomed silence one morning that let the townspeople know their well-liked piper had died.

He had fallen from a cart outside of town the previous evening and broken his neck. He was the last of Kirkwall's town pipers. It is not known whether Jamie had taken a dram the night he died but, like so many other pipers, then and now, he would toss off a dram with the best of them. Sometimes, in his cups, Jamie would hold forth on the other aspect of his talents. He was one of those rare characters who could commune with the dead, though he never attempted to profit from this skill in any way. He could commune with the spirits virtually at will and, after a dram or two, was happy to talk of the delights of heaven. A drink or two more and he would tell of the misery and despair of those denizens of the other place – hell. Like many of his name he claimed descent from Scotland's great hero, William Wallace, though as with many others the claim was hardly capable of absolute proof. When he died, the townspeople tried to have another piper appointed in his place but the council refused point-blank. However, he was long remembered and a local poet left an elegy to him:

Kirkwallians list to what I tell
He's gone from you who bore the bell;
He's gone, whose notes awoke the morn
And to his narrow house he's borne.

St Magnus still may tell the time
But he'll not now prolong the chime;
No more will Jamie take the round
For low he lies beneath the ground.

He had his faults, but let them rest
Faults stick to characters the best;
Of this I'm sure that Kirkwall town
Has lost a piper of renown.

The Luck o Geordie

Now, Geordie MacPhee was a travelling man. He, his wife and their two children lived on the road, just as their ancestors had since time beyond memory. Like most of the travellers, Geordie could turn his hand to many things; the tinkers are, after all, so called because they were, for a while at least in their history, travelling tin-smiths. But what liked most of all was to play the pipes. Geordie and many a summer was spent travelling through Scotland with his family, living wherever they could and getting money from the piping. In the winter, like many travellers, he and his wife would try and find some kind of house so they could send their bairns to the school – for they wanted to make sure the young ones would be able to read and write when they grew up. For generations travellers kept the oral traditions going as part of their distinctive culture, but more and more they realised that in the modern world their children would be disadvantaged if they couldn't read and write. So the plan was always to try and get a place to stay through the worst months of the year.

This particular year, however, they were still on the road when the weather broke and the winter was upon them. There was Geordie carrying a big pack of stuff and his pipes, his two young laddies with smaller packs, and their mother pushing a pram with a pile of bedclothes and the like piled on top. They carried everything they had, and just about everything they needed, with them as they went.

Now, it was dark and getting cold and so Mag said to him: 'C'mon, Geordie, where are we gonna go the night?'

'Ah,' he said, 'a puckle miles down the road there's an auld smiddy, right beside the road. It's no been used for years and we likely can stay there; we'll get some sticks, maybe the rafters even, and we'll get a fire goin and give the bairns a bite to eat, all right.' So they went on for another bit and, sure enough, there by the road was the old smiddy. Now, it was in a right tumbledown state and had no windows at all; the gaps were closed with canvas bags, and Geordie realised somebody else had been staying there off and on. This was all to the good as it meant the place was probably wind-proof at least. So in they went and found a pile of straw in one corner; he said, 'That straw's fine and clean for sleepin on – it looks like somebody's been dossin here before.'

They got their bedclothes and made a nice sleeping area on the straw and Geordie set to looking for sticks to make a fire. First he broke some sticks off the rafters and then he made a fire. They boiled up water for tea and Mag got out a pot, which she filled up with tatties and some mutton she had got from a farm on the road; pretty soon a nice smell was filling the place.

Once the wee lads had eaten, they fell straight asleep; they were used to the outdoor life but it was really cold that time. Geordie was sitting with his feet at the fire, smoking on his pipe, when Mag said, 'Well, that's me, I'm for ma bed as well. Good night, Geordie.'

'Aye, fine,' he grunted, looking deep into the flickering flames. A while later he took off his boots and his breeks and climbed into bed, still smoking away. When he heard a funny sound; it was a scuffling noise, so he sat up and looked towards the door, where the noise came from. There was a man coming in towards the fire. He was just in his stocking feet, his braces were hanging down over his trousers and all he had on his upper body was a shirt.

He looked down at Geordie. 'Ye're no scared are ye?' the man asked.

'No, I'm no scared,' replied Geordie, wondering what was going on. Now, he wasn't in the least scared because he'd been brought up as a fighting man and in all his life he had never been beaten by anyone. He reckoned whatever happened he would be able to take care of himself.

'Well,' said the stranger, 'I'd like ye to come and follow me.'

'No. I dinnae think so,' replied Geordie, as calm as you like.

'It's a real cold night and I'm a bit tired, so I'm just goin to go aff to sleep. Maybe some other time!'

As he said that, the man turned and went out through the door, into the wild night. Now, as Geordie went off to sleep he began to think he must have dozed off and been dreaming. Nobody would be going about dressed like that in this kind of weather. Thinking that, he drifted into a deep and easy sleep.

When he awoke in the morning, Mag was up and already had the fire going to make some tea.

'Morning, Geordie, I think we'd better get packed up and try and get on a bit once we've had our tea.'

So he got up and had a look outside. By now the snow was easily a foot deep and he turned to Mag and said, 'No, I think we'll stay here another nicht; I dinnae fancy goin on in this.'

So they had some tea and some food and Geordie thought it would be a good thing if he went around the farm towns nearby and played his pipes. He'd maybe get some money or some food for them all. So he went round the farms nearby and played his pipes and, sure enough, he came back with a few shillings, some bread and other stuff. They all had a fine feed and the same thing happened as the night before. Geordie was the last one awake. He was lying beside Mag and the bairns, smoking, when he heard the funny noise again. He turned and looked over his shoulder and there was the same man, in his stocking feet with his braces hanging over his trousers.

'Ye're no scared, are ye?' asked the stranger.

'No, I'm no scared, what for should a man like myself be scared?' he said.

'Right then,' said the stranger, 'will ye rise and follow me?'

'Ach, why not?' smiled Geordie. 'Aye, I'll follow ye. But will ye tell me whaur we are goin?'

'I will tell ye that it'll be warth yer while, I promise,' said the stranger.

'OK,' said Geordie.' Just let me get ma breeks and boots on.'

173

He put on his trousers and fastened his boots, then followed the man out through the door. As they went out, Geordie lifted his coat and hung it over his shoulders.

Out they went to the back of the house and over a little fence, then over a field till they were overlooking the sea. The man turned around and said, 'Now we're goin doun tae the beach and the rocks are gey slippy, so be careful now.'

'Right you are, lead on,' replied Geordie and the pair of them went down to the shore. They got down a rocky path to the shore and the tide was out. As they headed along the beach Geordie asked the man, 'Now where is it ye're takin me?'

The man stopped and turned around, 'Well I'll tell ye if ye like. Ye're sure you're no scared?'

'No, I tellt ye, I'm no scared,' said Geordie, though by now he well knew that this was no human he was out with on a dark winter's night by the seashore. But, as he said, he wasn't scared, just interested. He spoke again: 'I'm no scared but I tell ye I'm goin no further till ye tell me a bit more. Ye've said it would be worth ma while tae follow ye and I've done that, but what are we down here on the shore for? What are we supposed to be here for?'

The man looked long at him. Then he spoke. 'Jist along the beach there's a wee cave and I want you to come into the cave and . . .' he hesitated briefly, 'I'll give ye a fortune.'

'Right,' said Geordie, 'on ye go.'

So the man went on and within a minute or two they were at the mouth of a cave.

'I havnae got a match,' the stranger said.

'Well, I aye carry a bit candle wi me,' said Geordie, feeling in one of the many pockets in his greatcoat. He fished out a half a candle and a match.

'On ye go, then,' said the man and Geordie walked into the cave with his candle. The man came and stood behind him as the candle threw flickering light on the walls of the cave.

'Now look down,' the stranger said. 'Do ye see that big flagstone there?'

'It would be hard to miss,' Geordie said back.

'Well, underneath that there's a fortune in gold. Ye're a man with a wife an two kiddies, and a tramp on the road if I'm seein right. Ye're the only man that's ever been brave enough to follow me down here; I've asked more than a few and not a one of them that wasnae scared to follow me in the night. Ye're a brave man right enough.'

'Well, fine,' said Geordie, thinking that maybe this was a worthwhile thing to be doing, 'I'll have a go and see if I can shift this flagstone.' So he put the candle end on a nearby rock and bent to try and move the flagstone. At that point he realised that he was alone. The man had disappeared.

So, by the flickering light of a candle in a cave by the shore Geordie McPhee began to try and move the flagstone. First, he dug around it with his hands so he could get a purchase on the edge. Then, squatting over the great stone, he grabbed it with both hands and pulled. He strained till the sweat broke out on his brow; then all at once the flagstone moved. It slid from his grasp and fell into the hole below. Geordie stuck his hands into the bottom of the hole, below where the great stone had rested. His fingers touched something hard and round, then another, then another, and then even more. He grabbed three or four of the objects and pulled them out to look at them by the light of the candle. Gold sovereigns! Taken aback, he dropped the coins and heard them clink against more down in the hole. So he got on his knees and began to fill his pockets with the gold.

Once his pockets were bulging, he dragged the flagstone out and over the hole again. Then he headed back up to the smiddy, trouser- and coat-pockets filled with gold. He crept into the smiddy, got undressed and climbed into the bed on the straw. As he fell asleep, he was smiling with the thought that it had been a profitable night's work.

He awoke just as the feeble morning light of winter began to streak the sky. He got the fire started and put water on to boil. He awoke Mag and told her to get some food on while he hunted through his bag. He found what he was looking for right away – an old open razor. He took some of the water from the pot and began to shave himself as Mag looked on with a puzzled look.

'Where are ye goin that ye need tae shave, Geordie?' she asked.

'I'm away down to the town,' he said. 'There's a couple o things I need tae see to.'

'And what would be those couple o things ?' enquired Mag, by now sensing something was up.

'Well, I'm goin to have myself a drink, then I'll buy us some grub and I'll come back an we can feed the bairns,' came the reply.

'Where will ye get the money for that?' Mag asked. 'Are ye takkin yer pipes tae try an make some?'

'Och, wheesht, woman,' he snapped, 'dinnae ask so many questions. I'm just goin into the toun tae get some messages, all right!'

Off he went into the town. As he got near to the town he saw a big house with a long front drive, just to the left of the road. He peered over the fence; there was a man clearing the snow off the drive. Behind the man was a big board, which said, 'Property for Sale'. Now Geordie couldn't read, so he asked the man, who he thought was a gardener or something, 'What does it say on thon board there, man?'

The gardener looked at him, at the board and back at Geordie again. He shrugged his shoulders; 'It says "For Sale". The big house there is on the market.'

'Oh aye,' said Geordie, 'an how much would they be wantin for that fine big house?'

'Well,' said the man, leaning on his shovel, 'it's not just the house. There's quite a lot of land as well; it's a small estate, so they'll be asking thousands of pounds for it, I should think. Aye, it'll cost a wee fortune to buy the laird's estate, I'm thinking.'

'Tell me, then,' said Geordie, scratching his smooth chin, 'where would I find this mannie, the laird?'

'Och, he's down in London the now,' the man said.

'Well, who should I see if I wanted to buy this house and land?' enquired Geordie. Now, the man knew fine Geordie was a traveller and was sure he had no intention of buying the house, but he had nothing better to do than sweep snow so he decided to humour Geordie.

'Well, if you were looking to buy the laird's house your best bet would be to go and see Mr McRitchie in the village. He's the laird's lawyer.'

'Right then, I will,' said Geordie moving off. 'Thanks for your time, mannie.'

He went into the town – really it wasn't much more than a big village and he started asking people where he could find Mr McRitchie. But before he went to see the lawyer man he nipped into the local pub and had a dram or two. After a while he came out and found a wee local lad to take him to McRitchie's house.

McRitchie came to his door when he heard a knock. He was a wee, stocky old man with glasses and when he opened his door he was a bit taken aback. Geordie, living as he did, wasn't what you would call well-dressed: his toes were just about peeking through the fronts of his boots, his old greatcoat was tattered and torn and his breeks had clearly seen better days. The only thing half-way respectable about him was the fact that he had shaved and washed his face.

McRitchie took one look at Geordie and said, 'No. I've nothing for you today and I have no need of anything either. Good-bye.' And he shut the door straight in Geordie's face. Now this is the kind of treatment travellers have been getting since Noah was a lad and it didn't put Geordie off at all. He thought the man a bit rude but didn't let it bother him. He simply waited a few minutes and knocked again.

When McRitchie came back to the door and saw Geordie still standing there he got into a rage. 'What are you still doing here?' he shouted. 'If you don't get away from my door I'll call the police.'

'Haud yer horses,' said Geordie. 'I'm only here to ask about the big house you're sellin for the laird.'

Now, the lawyer fellow thought that Geordie was a bit wrong in the head. Why would a dirt poor tinker be wanting to ask about a great big house like that? He must be mad. So he decided to humour him a bit.

'Ah, you're interested in the house are you? Just you stay here and I'll nip down to the office and get the title deeds and other papers. Just stay here; I won't be long.'

Then he headed into the town and in a few minutes Geordie could see him coming back up. But he wasn't alone; there were two other men with him. Two men in blue uniforms. Two police-man, a sergeant and a constable.

The three of them came up to where Geordie was standing.

'This is the man. He's been tormenting me all day,' piped the lawyer. 'Get him out of here; he's not right in the head.'

'Come on, now,' said the sergeant, 'just you come along wi us. Ye've been botherin Mr McRitchie and disturbin the peace; a night in the jail will calm you down. Come along.'

Now, Geordie was a man who had a temper and he certainly wasn't scared of two big soft polis. 'Look,' he said, 'I came here to ask about the house that's for sale – the estate at the edge o the town – and I want to find out how much it'll cost me to buy it.'

The sergeant thought he was taking the mick, and was about to pull out his truncheon when the young constable with him butted in. 'Are you serious? You? You want to buy the laird's estate?' he demanded with a look of absolute disbelief.

'Aye, that's it exactly,' said Geordie, still keeping his temper under control. 'I want to see how much it is.'

Standing there as calm as you like, despite the way he was dressed, made the others stop and think a bit.

'The house is for sale, right?' the sergeant asked McRitchie.

'It most certainly is but . . .' the lawyer began.

'Well then, why don't you ask him in to discuss it?' said the sergeant with a funny smile. Geordie knew right away what was going on. The sergeant wanted him inside the house and would then arrest him for breaking and entering or something else. That way they would be able to get him stuck in the jail for few years. Still, he thought, I've come this far, so let's try a bit more.

So into the house they trooped. The lawyer, the two polis and Geordie. Now Geordie didn't put a foot wrong. He followed the lawyer into a big front room and sat at a big table while McRitchie took out a heap of papers from his briefcase. The two policemen were watching, ready to pounce if Geordie even breathed in the wrong direction, but they were in for a shock.

MacRitchie told Geordie the price, expecting him to get up and try to run out of the house. And the price was quite a few thousand pounds.

'Well,' says Geordie, 'I cannae give you it all just now, but what about a deposit?'

And he reached into his pockets and brought out a great big pile of shiny sovereigns. 'You'll have an idea what these are worth will ye?' he asked with a wee smile.

At the sight of the sovereigns the jaws of both policemen had dropped, but the wee lawyer's eyes lit up, just as you would expect. McRitchie counted the coins and made a few notes.

'That's fine for a deposit,' he said. 'How will you pay the rest?'

'Och, I'll come back tomorrow with the rest,' he said. 'Just the same, cash on the barrel.' Now this was of course music to the lawyer's ears. They are never happier than when counting other people's money, to see how much they can get to keep for themselves, but the two policemen were dumbfounded, the sergeant particularly so. It's one thing picking on a travelling man, but when that man appears to be really rich – the truth is, he couldn't understand what was going on at all. So the policemen left and Geordie followed on behind them, after shaking the lawyer by the hand and arranging to come back the following day. He went into the town and had a couple of drinks in the pub, went and bought food for his family and headed back to the smiddy.

When he got back, he and Mag and the bairns had a right good feed. Then Geordie sat down to wait. He didn't want to go down to the beach till after dark. That was how it had worked before and he didn't want to take any chances on maybe breaking the spell. Better safe than sorry, he was thinking. So that night he went back down to the cave on the beach, this time with a sack. He went into the cave and filled the sack as full as he could and still be able to carry it, for gold sovereigns weigh quite a bit. Then up with the gold and back to the smiddy. He left the sack outside the building, sure that nobody was going to come near.

The following morning after some breakfast he left Mag and the kids and headed back into the town to see the lawyer. Well, how his eyes lit up when Geordie poured out the gold on his desk.

'I've never seen so much gold in all my life,' he said. 'There's more than enough here to buy the house and the land that goes with it. More than enough.' Some of the coins had rolled off the desk onto the floor and Geordie bent down and started picking them up.

'Well, I suppose you'll want to put the rest of the money in the bank?' asked the lawyer.

'Naw, naw,' said Geordie, 'I dinnae hae time for banks. Dinnae trust them. How's about you look after them for me?'

'Well, if you're sure,' McRitchie said dubiously, 'but the money would be better in the bank.'

'Nope,' said Geordie,' you're my mannie now and you sign everything about the house and just look after the money as well, OK? And here take some o this money for yourself.'

At that he handed the lawyer a large handful of the gold coins.

'Very good, sir,' replied the lawyer. 'That's just how we'll do it, sir.'

'What for are ye callin me sir?' asked Geordie, 'My name is Geordie MacPhee – there's nae need to call me sir. Geordie MacPhee, that's me.'

'All right then, Geordie MacPhee,' the lawyer smiled. 'We'll see that we get everything arranged just the way you want it, sir.' You see, the lawyer couldn't help himself. Normally, of course, he would never call any traveller sir, though he might call them a lot of other things, but the sight of all that money had confused him. Lawyers are like that; money always seems to excite them.

'Now, stop cryin me sir,' Geordie said, 'my name is Geordie MacPhee.' At that he turned and walked out of the room. Immediately, McRitchie was on his feet following him into the lobby.

'Just one second, sir, eh, I mean Mr MacPhee,' he half-stuttered, 'there's something I want you to do.'

'Well, what?' demanded Geordie.

'I think you should go to the tailor shop in the town and get yourself a new suit of clothes,' MacRitchie said with a smile. 'You can't really go about in those rags, now that you have money and land.'

'Well, I've never had a new suit o clothes in all my life,' Geordie said, beginning to think, 'but can you get me a suit of clothes to fit me just right?'

'I tell you what I'll do,' replied the lawyer, 'I'll get the tailor to come over now and measure you up for a suit right here.'

A few minutes later, after a phone call, the tailor turned up and measured Geordie for a new suit. Whatever he thought of it all, he said nothing; this might be a traveller, but he had money, so he'd just get on with his job.

Within a couple of days Geordie had his new suit, and he looked pretty good in it, especially once he had got himself a new shirt and a pair of boots. The next thing was to get Mag and the lads kitted out as well. So he told the lawyer this was what he wanted and McRitchie said he would arrange it.

'You'll have to tell me where you're staying, so we can arrange to have them picked up,' the lawyer said.

Och, we've been stayin in the old smiddy out on the west road,' Geordie told him. 'It's a bit cold though.'

'Well,' said the wee lawyer, 'we'll get the chauffeur to take you out in the Rolls. There's also a Buick and Humber up at the big house but the Rolls is far and away the best, sir. You'll get a fine hurl in that car; it never let the other gentleman down.'

'Sounds all right to me,' said Geordie. 'How do we get hold of this chauffeur mannie?'

'I'll just phone him now,' McRitchie replied.

'Right then, tell him to pick me up in the pub in an hour. I fancy wettin ma whistle,' said Geordie, and headed off to the pub.

Now, by the time that the car turned up at the bar, Geordie had already bought everybody there two or three drinks and the place was jumping. Geordie was having another nip with the publican, who was well gone, when the 'beep beep' of the car sounded outside.

'Right,' said Geordie, 'that's me, I'm off.'

He came out of the bar to find the chauffeur standing to attention with the rear door of the Rolls Royce held open. Geordie handed the chauffeur the bottle of beer he had in his hand. 'Here, have a slug,' he offered.

'Och, no, sir, I couldn't. Not when I'm driving,' the man replied.

'Ach, just have a wee slug,' Geordie insisted, shoving the bottle into the man's hand. So the chauffeur had a wee sip of the beer.

'Right,' Geordie said, 'let's go. Have ye got the parcels that I bought yesterday?'

'Yes, sir, they're all in the back,' the chauffeur replied.

'Stop callin me sir,' shouted Geordie. 'My name is Geordie MacPhee and I used to play my pipes for money on the streets o this town, and only a wee whilie ago as well. Dinna call me sir.'

He then looked close at the chauffeur. 'How much are ye paid?'

'Well, I receive five pounds a week, plus my keep,' the man said.

'Ach, tae hang wi that,' laughed Geordie. 'I've plenty money. I'll gie ye ten pound a week, all right.'

Now, this pleased the chauffeur and from then on he couldn't do enough for Geordie. They went and bought more food and drink, put it all in the back of the Rolls Royce and headed off towards the big house.

'Hoi, hang on,' shouted Geordie from the back seat, 'we're no goin to the big house. We're to go to the old smiddy out on the west road; ye know where that is?'

'Well, sir, I thought we should get a couple of the woman servants to come out with us and see to your wife,' said the chauffeur, keen to help in any way he could. 'And we have a nanny up at the house and she could look after the laddies,' he added.

'Och, that's good thinkin,' replied Geordie. So by the time they got to the smiddy, there was Geordie and the chauffeur in the Rolls, followed by the Humber with two men and two women as well as the young nanny to look after the wee lads.

When the Rolls Royce came rolling up to the smiddy Mag saw it comin and shouted to the laddies: 'Come here quick boys here's an important mannie comin up the road in a big car. Somebody must hae seen ye breakin that hedge ower there; we'll all be for it now.'

Just at that, the car door opened and out stepped Geordie, a bottle of beer in his hand and a great big smile on his face.

'Well, are ye ready to go to the new house, Mag?' he asked, grinning furiously.

'My God,' stuttered Mag, 'is that you Geordie MacPhee?'

'Aye, it certainly is, Mag,' he said, 'and here's a couple o women here wi a lot o new clothes for you and the laddies. They'll help get you kitted out.'

Poor Mag was totally stunned by what was happening and allowed herself to be taken back into the smiddy, where the maids helped her into new clothes. The two laddies were also kitted out in the finest of new gear, after getting a good scrubbing – laddies, no matter whether they're travellers, poor folk or the children of the rich, can always be relied on to gather a fair bit of dirt.

Once all three of them were properly kitted out, the two men came to take them out to the car. At this, Mag broke out of the spell she seemed to be under and backed off, shouting, 'Geordie, there's two shan gadgies after me.'

Geordie stuck his head round the smiddy doorway. 'Ach, dinnae fash. They're no shan gadgies, they work for us; they're all right. Come on.'

Geordie got into the car, and Mag, pulling away from the two men who had taken her by the arms, tripped into the car, falling all her length. This tickled Geordie, especially when the two laddies climbed over their prostrate mother and into the back of the Rolls Royce. They were delighted with the motor and chattered away happily to each other about how grand it was. Then off they went to the new house.

One of the laddies asked the chauffeur in the front, 'Hey, mannie, is it hard to drive this thing?'

'Ach, wheesht, boy,' shouted Geordie (by this time he was well on) 'leave the mannie alone. If ye distract him we'll maybe end up drivin intae a dyke or somethin. Just wheesht the nou.' And he burst into a few verses of song while Mag sat there, bemused and looking around her at the car, at her own and the laddies' new clothes and, most of all, at her man.

When they got to the big house the rest of the staff were lined up outside on the drive. The house was grand, almost like a castle in fact. So Geordie stepped out of the Rolls Royce with a great happy grin on his face.

'What's all this?' he asked the chauffeur.

'This is the rest of the staff, Geordie,' he said. 'They're lined up to meet their new employer, sir.'

'Och, will ye stop that cryin me sir,' roared Geordie, 'ye ken my name. Use it.'

He turned to the line of servants, just as Mag marched right past with the two laddies. But Geordie wanted to speak to the staff so he went down the line, asking them who they were and how much they were getting paid. Whenever anybody said, 'I am on four pounds a week,' he would reply, 'No, you're on eight.' And if they said, 'I am on ten pounds,' which a couple of them were, he said, 'No, ye're on twenty.' So he went down the line and the upshot was that all the staff, the servants in the house, the gardeners and the gamekeepers, all got their wages doubled. Now, they might have had reservations about a traveller taking over as laird but it was hard to feel upset when you had just had your wages doubled. The majority of them decided that they liked their new boss.

The next day was market day in the town and Geordie decided he couldn't miss this. It was always a fine thing to go and gave a drink on market day anywhere in the country, so he told the staff he was away down to the village. By the time he got to the front door the chauffeur was already there with the Rolls Royce, ready to take him to the town. But Geordie wasn't having any of that. He and Mag and the two laddies would walk down and enjoy the brisk clear day.

Geordie was looking pretty good in his brand new suit that day, but by the following day he was as scruffy as he ever was. He got blazing drunk at the market, buying everybody in sight drinks and spending a small fortune on buying horses. Now, some of the horses could have had three legs for all the worth they were, but Geordie didn't care a hoot. He was rich and he fancied buying horses. So he did. There were quite a lot of travellers there that day and Geordie made sure that they all had plenty to drink; he was handing out money hand over fist. So, as you would expect, a lot of them got pretty drunk, and by the late afternoon a few of them were staggering about the place. At this point, the police came on the scene and started rounding them up. It was the same sergeant and constable that Geordie had met when he arrived. As they were taking a couple of the men off to the jail, Geordie came over. The policemen stopped what they were doing, and saluted Geordie. Drunk as they were, the two fellows who had been lifted were impressed!

'Good day, sir,' the sergeant began.

'Aye, aye,' said Geordie, 'what are ye doin with these lads here?'

'Well, sir, they're drunk and incapable so we're taking theme to the cells to sober up and we'll let them go in the morning,' the sergeant replied.

'No, just leave them alone. All right? It's me that's been buying their drink an I'll stand responsibility for them,' said Geordie, enjoying himself.

'Well, if you say so, sir,' the policeman replied dubiously.

'I'll make sure there's no trouble, officer, all right,' Geordie went on.

'Right you are then, sir.' The two policeman saluted and went off. By the time it was dark there were quite a few drunk travellers and, although some of them were staying nearby, most of them were in no fit state to get back to where they had camped.

'Ach,' said Geordie when he realised what was going on, 'I'll get them all covers for the night.'

By now the whole town knew how rich this traveller fellow was; so when Geordie wanted to get the ironmonger's shop opened to get tarpaulins and other stuff for the other travellers to put up benders on his land, there was no problem at all. They got the horses he had bought and carried the covers and poles and everything else back up to the big house and put up the benders.

Not at the back of the house in the fields, but right there on the front lawn of the big house the benders were built. As soon as the snow was cleared and the benders up, fires were started; within a short time it was like a tent city. Fires were burning, the wood coming from bushes and trees on the estate; children were running around, men were playing the pipes and generally a good time was being had by all. Dogs were running all over the place and bairns were up to all sorts of tricks. So pretty soon the front lawn and the gardens around it were in a right mess.

At last, Geordie, after playing a good few tunes himself, went up into the big house and into his bed. When he woke up in the morning and looked out, his bonny front lawn was a right mess with all the ashes of the fires and the benders all over the place. Some of the travellers got up and left and others were hanging around to see what would happen next when a big car came up to the front door. It was McRitchie.

He came into the house and he and Geordie sat down at the kitchen table while Mag made some tea for them. 'Well, sir,' began the lawyer, 'I have none of your money left and, of course, you have nothing in the bank, so I was just wondering what you are going to do now.'

Geordie smiled, 'Dinnae ye worry about that; I'll get you plenty money.' So the lawyer went away and, that night, being careful no one saw him, Geordie went back down to the cave on the beach for more gold. But he had been throwing the gold about like confetti and there wasn't that much left. He was making some money by selling the horses he had paid too much for, and there was some more coming in from the estate, but his outgoings were way above his income and the supply of sovereigns was getting dangerously low. Still, he had some left so Geordie refused to let things bother him.

A few days after the market day another big car came up to the door. Here, wasn't it the previous owner and his wife coming to introduce themselves to the new laird!

'My word,' said the woman, stepping out of the car. 'What a dreadful sight. The place looks terrible. Whatever is going on?'

Her husband, the old laird, got out after her and said, 'Good God, what in thunder has been happening here? The place is a disgrace!'

They came up the front stairs and there at the door was Mag.

'Would ye be wantin a cup of tea?' she says to the woman in a friendly tone, 'and I've got some tatties on for a bite to eat. Come away in; it's right cauld out here.'

She took the woman by the shoulder to bring her in, but the woman shrugged her off with a look of real horror. 'Who is this creature?' she shrieked at her husband.

Just then Geordie himself came to the door, with a bottle in his hand.

'Would you like a drink, mannie?' he said, holding the bottle out to the well-dressed man before him.

The man took one look at the bottle – cheap sherry, as Geordie's money was getting scarce – and shuddered.

'Good God, no. This is just too horrible,' he said. 'Come on, Gisela, let's go; we can't stay here with these . . . these people.'

'Right ye are then,' shouted Geordie, 'bugger off and dinnae come back.' The pair of them scampered back to their car and drove away at speed, leaving Geordie and Mag at the door of their new home.

Well, the cheap sherry gave it away, you see. Geordie had got rid of a fortune in gold in just a matter of a few weeks. A few days later he went into the town to see McRitchie and tell him that he didn't have the money to keep the estate going. He was broke.

'It's no wonder,' said McRitchie. 'You've been handing money out hand over fist. I hear you've even bought some of your traveller friends new cars?'

'Aye, I did,' said Geordie.

'Well, I notice that they've all gone off and left you with nothing, while their pockets are full of your money. About the only income you have is the deer-shooting and the few cattle and sheep you have left. Well, you'll just have to sell them too.'

So Geordie hung on for a week or two more, but then he had to sell the whole estate. Now, he didn't get near what he had paid for it, as he had let things slide, but it was a fair amount of money. But it was no surprise to anyone when that money went just the way of his previous fortune and, soon enough, Geordie was flat broke again.

The following summer he came to the town with Mag and the lads to play his pipes, and many people were happy to buy him a drink in memory of the fun they had had the previous year. So Geordie went back on the road, playing his pipes and living out of doors, just as he had always done. But he made a point of coming back every year to play his pipes at the market and there is no doubt about it – he and Mag and the laddies always had a first-class time there.

Jock and his Bagpipes

There was this woman lived away out in the country and she had two sons, both called Jock. They got along all right; both the lads helped their mother about the house and looked after the few cattle they had. This went on for a few years until the eldest said one day, 'Mother, I think it's time I headed out into the world and made my fortune, whatever it will be.'

Now, the woman was sad that her son wanted to go off into the wide world, but she understood that it was the way of things that young men would want to go off and seek their fortune; he would go whether she wanted him to or not. So she told him to go to the nearby well and fetch some water and she would bake him a bannock to take with him.

'Now son,' she said, 'here's the wee dish and the sieve. The more water you bring me back from the well, the bigger a bannock I will be able to bake for you.' So Jock set off for the well and there, sitting on a rock by the well, was a little bird. As he came up to the well, the little bird piped up:

Stuff it with moss
And clog it with clay
And that will carry
The water away.

He was telling Jock that he could carry more water using the sieve than he could get in the dish alone, which was a bit small. But Jock was an impatient sort of lad and there was no way he would let himself be told what to do by a bird!

'No chance,' he said, 'there's no chance I'll let a bird tell me what to do. Away with you.'

So he went back to the house and his mother baked him a bannock to take with him when he set out to seek his fortune the next day. But as she only had the little water he had brought her, she could only make him a little bannock. He put the bannock into his pocket, said goodbye to his mother and little brother and went off out into the big world to find his fortune.

He had been walking for an hour or two and decided to sit down and eat when he noticed a bird – the same little bird that had been at the well. The bird came up to him and it said, 'If you give me a bit of your bannock, you can have a feather from my wing to make bagpipes.'

'Away with you. I've barely enough to feed myself here. Anyway, it was your fault I didn't get more water. Now shoo.'

And the little bird flew away.

On and on Jock walked till at last he saw a big house. 'Ahaa,' he thought, 'maybe I can get some work here.'

So he went up to the house and knocked on the door. After a little while the door opened and there stood a grey-haired, stern-looking woman, whom he assumed was the housekeeper of the place.

'What do you want?' she asked Jock.

'I am looking for work,' he replied. 'Do you have any work for a strong young lad?'

'Hmm,' she said, looking him up and down, 'what kind of work can you do?'

'Well,' Jock replied, 'I can carry ashes, wash dishes, dig the garden and I can herd cattle.'

'Herd cattle, can you? How do you think you would do herding hares?' the woman asked him, with an odd glint in her eye.

'I think I'd be all right,' replied Jock, thinking this was a bit strange; but he needed to work to eat.

'Well, then,' she said, smiling, 'if you can go down to the field and take care of the hares there and bring them all home tonight, you'll get the hand of the daughter of the house.'

Jock was thinking to himself, 'These must be tame hares. I can handle them.' It was the idea that he would get to marry the daughter of the owner of this big house that was exciting him. He thought if he could manage that he would have made his fortune, no trouble at all. He didn't even think what she would be like; he just thought that here was his chance to be something, at the very first place he had come to. He was excited, but didn't want to let on too much.

'Och well, ma'am. I think I could have a go at that,' he said.

So she sent him down to the field and there were twenty-four hares all running about, and one poor crippled one, sitting all on its own. Jock thought to himself that this would be easy; he sat down on a stone by the gate of the field to watch over the hares. Now, after a while he began to feel a bit peckish – all he'd had to eat all day was the little bannock his mother had baked him. His stomach was rumbling with hunger and he thought to himself that nobody would miss the crippled hare, especially as none of the other hares were coming anywhere near it. He was the sort of lad who only ever thought of his own needs and rarely about the consequences of his actions.

So he simply grabbed the crippled hare, snapped its neck, gutted it and made a fire to roast it. It only took a few minutes. While he was doing this he was thinking about filling his belly and didn't notice that the rest of the hares saw what he was doing and disappeared into the walls of the field and hid. When nightfall came he looked all round the field and in all the other fields close by, but not one hare could he find. They were all hiding in gaps in the field dykes and in holes in the ground and he had no idea at all where any of them were. So he went back up to the big house. When the people there found out that he had not brought back the hares, they up and hanged him, just like that. Some fortune he had made.

Meanwhile, back at the wee farmhouse, his little brother, also called Jock, began to think that he too should go out into the world and seek his fortune. He was a kindly lad, but he was fed up just living on this lonely farm and wanted to see what the world was like. He was also missing his brother, even if they hadn't always got on too well. He felt he needed to go out into the wide world and meet new people, see new things and go to new places. So he too told his mother that he wanted to go out and seek his fortune in the world.

Now, the woman was even sadder that her second son wanted to go off into the wide world and leave her all on her own. But she understood that this was the way of things and that he would go whether she wanted him to or not. So she told him to go to the well and fetch some water and she would bake him a bannock to take with him.

'Now, son,' she said, 'here's the wee dish and the sieve. The more water you bring me back from the well, the bigger a bannock I will be able to bake for you.' So Jock set off for the well and there, sitting on a rock by the well, was a little bird. As he got came to the well, the little bird piped up:

Stuff it with moss
And clog it with clay

And that will carry
The water away.

'Thank you very much,' said Jock, 'that's a really good idea; I'll just do that.'

So he took moss and clay and stuck it all round the inside of the sieve. This meant that, with the sieve and the wee dish full, he took a pretty decent amount of water back to his mother.

'Oh, Jock,' she smiled, when he got back to the house, 'well done. I'll make you a fine big bannock to take with you on your way in the morning.'

So in the morning Jock got up and kissed his mother; she gave him the great big bannock she had baked for him and sent him off on his way with her blessing.

Well, he wasn't all that far along the road when he began to feel a little peckish and sat down to eat. He had just broken a piece off the big bannock, and was about to put it into his mouth, when he saw the little bird he had seen the day before at the well.

'Hello,' said the little bird. 'That's a fine big bannock. If you give me piece of it, I'll let you pull a feather out of my wing and make a set of bagpipes from it.'

'Now, that would be a good trick to see,' replied Jock. 'I've plenty to eat here, so I'm happy to give you a piece of my bannock.' The bird took a piece of the bannock and swallowed it down.

'Now,' she said, 'pull a feather from my wing and it'll make a set of bagpipes.'

'Och,' said Jock, 'I wouldn't want to hurt you.'

'Never you mind about hurting me,' said the bird, a bit sternly. 'Just do as I tell you.'

Jock did as he was told and pulled a feather from the bird's wing. And didn't it turn into a lovely set of bagpipes right there before his eyes! He realised the bird had magic powers, but it was friendly and it had given him this fine set of bagpipes and some good advice already, so he thought he had nothing to worry about. He was quite delighted with the bagpipes and, after thanking the bird, went on his way along the road, playing a bright and cheery tune to himself. The bird flew off to the top of a nearby tree and watched as the young lad walked out of sight, playing happily on the bagpipes.

On and on he went till he came in sight of a fine big house. Well, he thought to himself, maybe I can find a bit of work here and make myself some money. So he went straight up to the house and knocked on the door.

When the housekeeper answered, he asked if there was any work.

'And what kind of work can you do?' the woman asked with a serious look.

'Och, all kinds of things about the house – cleaning and so on. And I'm a dab hand at looking after cattle and other beasts.'

'Well, you do think you could take care of hares?' she asked him.

'I've never done that before,' replied Jock honestly, 'but I am sure I can give it a go. What are the wages?' The woman looked at him with a strange glint in her eye. 'If you take care of the hares and bring them all back tonight, you'll get to marry the daughter of the master of this house. But if you fail, you'll be hanged!'

Jock was a bit taken aback at this, but he thought, 'How hard can it be looking after some hares?'

So he was sent down to the field and there were twenty-four hares bounding around and a crippled one half-sitting, half-lying on the ground. The hares that were running around all stopped and looked at Jock, who swung his pipes up to his lips and played them a tune. At this, they all began to leap about again. Most of the day passed with Jock playing away and the hares leaping about, with the one crippled creature looking as if it were listening to every note. After a while, Jock began to feel peckish, so he stuck his hand in his pocket and pulled out the last piece of the big bannock his mother had baked him and had it for his tea. When it came time to go back up to the big house, Jock led the hares up the road, gently carrying the poor little one that was crippled.

When he got back to the house the housekeeper and the master were delighted to see him, and they were delighted to hear him play his bagpipes for them. It wasn't long before he was married to the daughter of the house. And wasn't she a happy and very pretty lass at that. In the fullness of time, when the master of the house died, who should take his place but our Jock. And he lived a long and happy life, playing the magic bagpipes every day.

Fighting Tales

———◆———

T he role of the pipes in warfare was significant. Highland regiments of the British army followed an ancient tradition when they marched into battle with pipers at their head. As we saw in the story 'MacCrimmon Will Never Return', such a position was dangerous and the pipers were considered particularly brave men. We have already had some battles, but the first two tales here reflect a stubborn commitment that led to tragedy. The third story combines the widespread clan activity of cattle-raiding with a fine example of clear thinking under stress.

The Reel o Tulloch

There are various stories told of how this famous old tune arose; this one is from Strathspey.

Seumas Grant was a man of some standing in Strathspey. He had land, a good wife, plenty cattle and a growing family. Like all men of his time, he was adept with weapons, and like all Highlanders, was a proud man. He already had several sons when his wife, Jean, fell pregnant again. She was hoping for a daughter, and so, truth to tell, was Seumas. The day of the birth came round and Jean gave birth to a beautiful wee lassie, who they called Iseabail Dubh, Dark Isabel. In those days, and for long, long after, howdies looked after women giving birth. Now, the howdies were midwives, but were often more than just that. They helped with births and they laid out corpses after death and there

196

were many of them who had great wisdom and knowledge. Some of them were believed to be spae wives – women who had the power of prophecy and could see far into the future. It was one such howdie who officiated at Iseabail's birth.

'Take care, Mrs Grant,' she told her before taking her leave, 'take care wi this lass. She will be the cause of great tragedy if she isn't kept clear of a man as dark as herself.'

Now, in those days most people in Scotland were well aware that people who had mysterious powers often saw things others couldn't, and Jean pressed the woman to tell her more. 'I have no more to tell ye than that, Mrs Grant. Keep her away from any man as dark as herself.' Saying that, she left.

Iseabail grew up, tall and strong and beautiful, with olive skin, deep dark eyes, bright red lips and hair as black as a raven's wing. She was very much doted on by her father; it would be fair to say she wanted for nothing and was a bit spoilt. Her mother never forgot the howdie's words but, with the passing of time, they didn't seem quite so alarming. Maybe things would just settle down and be all right, Jean told herself.

And so Iseabail developed into a proud, beautiful and headstrong young woman. As she came into full womanhood her beauty was such that it was believed she could take her pick of any man in Strathspey, if not the whole of Scotland.

One day she was with her parents at the Ruthven fair. She was walking off on her own when she saw a handsome young man playing the pipes. Iain MacGregor was his name – Iain Dubh, Dark Ian – and he was a grand piper. As soon as she saw this six-foot tall Highlandman, just turned twenty, in traditional dress with sword and pistols at his belt, walking up and down as he played a march, her heart was won. His hair, like his beard, was jet black and his eyes were deep and dark. Now, Iseabail had heard of the prophecy at her birth but, headstrong as she was, she had decided it was superstitious rubbish. She saw this beautiful man and knew right off that he had to be hers.

Iain Dubh MacGregor hardly knew what hit him. One minute he was walking up and down through the fair, playing his pipes, then all at once a vision stepped in front of him. The most beautiful female he had ever seen stood right in front of him, staring boldly into his eyes and blushing furiously. The blood rushed to his cheeks as he looked into those deep dark eyes and his breath shortened.

'I am Iseabail Grant,' she said in a deep voice that sent shivers up and down his spine. 'Who are you?'

Stepping back, he gave the gorgeous creature a sweeping bow and replied, 'I am Iain MacGregor. They call me Iain Dubh.'

'Well, they call me Iseabail Dubh,' she replied. Their eyes locked.

'Are you the one . . .' he began to ask.

'The one who is supposed to avoid dark-haired men? Aye, that's me, but what care I for old wives' tales? Do you believe in that sort of thing?' she asked him, with a mischievous twinkle in her beautiful eyes.

Like everyone else, Iain knew of the prophecy, but what did it matter compared to this vision of absolute loveliness here before him, and obviously interested in him. 'If ever I did, I do not now,' he smiled.

The two of them were standing there, smiling at each other, when Jean saw them. Running over, she dragged her daughter away from the handsome youth and scolded her. 'What do you think you are doing, Iseabail?' she demanded. 'Who was that man? You have never been introduced to him before.' All the fears aroused by the howdie's prophecy had come rushing back.

'Och, mother, isn't he handsome,' was all the reply she could get from the clearly smitten lass.

'He is not for you,' said her mother, fearing that she was already too late.

Iseabail was dragged off to join her father and, when Jean told Seumas what had happened, he too was concerned – so concerned that he got in touch with Iain Dubh's father and suggested that the young lad be warned off. This was done, but it was all too late. No matter how hard both families tried, the two of them contrived to meet up with each other. Despite being watched constantly they managed to sneak away to find excitement and passion in each other's company. Iain was as skilled as any Highlander at travelling unseen through the countryside and he and Iseabail had several hiding places.

The situation was soon common knowledge, and people remembered the dire words of the howdie's prophecy all those years before. The woman had long had a reputation as a seer and on many occasion her words had been proved correct. So it happened that both clans, the Grants and MacGregors, agreed to put an end to the affair. The MacGregors themselves swore to ensure that the situation would stop. Iain was approached by two of his cousins, James Ban and Ewan Ruadh, on the orders of the chief and the elders of the MacGregor clan. He was told in no uncertain terms that if he did not stop seeing Iseabail Dubh Grant he would be killed.

'What are you telling me?' Iain replied in an ominously low voice.

'We are telling you to stop seeing the Grant girl, or else,' replied James Ban, his hand moving toward his sword.

'Listen to us,' interjected Ewan Ruadh. 'This is from the chief; you are to stop seeing the girl immediately.'

In those days, of course, all Highland warriors went around armed and Iain Dubh had long been known for being particularly good with the broadsword – the ancient two-handed battle weapon of the Highlanders. It took but a moment to whip the great weapon from over his shoulder – the fight was on.

His cousins were ready. They knew there was little chance of Iain giving in to their demand. They too were accomplished swordsmen but Iain, fired up with love and anger, was too quick and strong for them. Within a minute both his cousins lay dead in the road before him.

He had killed men of his own blood. Iain knew there was no choice but to flee; there would be no safety for him in Strathspey after this. Quickly, he headed home and gathered up his few possession – his pipes, his musket, powder and shot – and headed for the Grants' home. He told the go-between they had been using, a cousin of Iseabail's maid, to go and let her know what had happened and where she was to meet him. The lovers met in a barn at Tulloch and Iain told her the full story.

'I think things might get a bit rough,' she said, showing him that she too had brought a musket with plenty powder and ball.

'Has there ever been a woman like you?' he asked, and took her in his arms.

'Stop that, Iain, we have no time at the moment,' she said, pulling herself reluctantly from his grasp. 'There is but one possible way out of this, my love,' she said, holding his hands and looking into his eyes. 'We will have to be married as quickly as possible.'

'Oh, that is everything that I want Iseabail, but who will marry us now, after what I have done?' he asked.

'Ach, you know what they say: if you want something bad enough . . .'

Later that same day the minister at Kincardine was surprised to find two callers at his door. He recognised who they were.

'What is it you want?' he asked a bit warily.

Iain whipped out his dirk with lightning speed and held it tight against the minister's throat.

'Och, we were thinking you should marry us,' Iseabail said sweetly. Then, her voice hardening, she said, 'Right away. We don't have time to wait.'

Realising that the pair of them were absolutely serious in their intent, the poor minister had no choice but to comply. He called in his wife and their servant lass as witnesses, and there in the manse at Kincardine, Iseabail and Iain were married.

They were on their way back to the barn where they were hiding to celebrate their nuptials, when they looked down the glen. There, coming up the road towards them, was a crowd of men, about a dozen strong. They could clearly see that there were both Grants and MacGregors in the group: the clans had combined to hunt them down!

The young couple ran to the barn and barred the door with Iain's sword; Iseabail loaded the muskets. Through cracks in the barn walls they saw their kinsmen approaching, with drawn swords and muskets.

Iain shouted, 'Go back of all of you. Iseabail and I are now married. Leave us in peace or it will be the worse for you.'

The group stopped briefly, but came on. Their intention was clear.

On they came. Then a shot rang out, and another, and two men fell. The others raced to the barn but, before getting there, another one of them fell. It was difficult to aim at the attackers once they had closed on the barn and Iain threw down his musket and whipped his sword from across the door. The first man stumbled in and was killed instantly. He was a Grant. The next man through the door was a MacGregor, but Iain didn't hesitate and felled him too. Then there in the doorway stood Allan, Iseabail's brother, a look of hatred on his face.

Iseabail knelt on the ground with a loaded musket in her hands. 'Kill him Iain,' she cried, her voice breaking.

As the two men stood and looked at her, Iain shouted, 'I cannae kill yer brither, Iseabail!'

'It's you or him,' she cried. Iain still hesitated and Iseabail shouted in a tearful voice, 'If you don't kill him, I must. He's my brother – save me from having his blood on my hands.' Allan Grant flung himself at MacGregor. Iain stepped aside as Allan's sword whistled by him. Then he thrust with his great broadsword straight into Allan's heart. Behind Iain the remaining members of the group looked on in horror. They had heard what Iseabail had said and had seen the result. Putting up their weapons they turned in disgust and went off.

Iain, his blood up with the fervour of battle, picked up his pipes and strode up and down the barn composing a new tune as he went. This was the first time anyone ever heard the 'Reel o Tulloch'. He then put down his pipes and he and his new wife fell into each other's arms. Taking consolation in each other, aware they were now outcasts, they began to lay plans for getting out of Strathspey.

In the meantime they had to eat; Iain went out into the hills a couple of days later to kill a deer. Further discussion had been held between the MacGregors and the Grants. The MacGregors were in total agreement that Iain had to be caught and killed. So it was that, as he left to go hunting, Iain was watched and followed by a handpicked group of the finest fighting men of both clans.

The next thing Iseabail knew was several hours later, when a knock came on the barn door. Lifting a loaded musket, she gingerly opened the door.

There on the ground before her was the head of her lover and husband, Iain Dubh MacGregor! A mocking voice came from nearby: 'Look after your man, Iseabail – what's left of him.'

She shrieked in horror, and, picking up the head, ran off into the hills. Over the next few days she was seen in various locations kissing and cuddling the head of her man. She had clearly lost all reason. It was considered a relief all round when, a few days later, she was found dead on the hillside, still clutching the severed head of her man.

A Faithful Piper

Alexander MacColla MacDonald was a great fighter and leader of men. In the civil wars of the seventeenth century, provoked by the Stewart kings' attempts to impose their religion and absolute authority on the population of Scotland and England, he ended up on the royalist side. There are those who say that this was because he, like his father, the original Coll Citach, was more interested in regaining lost MacDonald lands on the Kintyre peninsula and the island of Islay than in any particular religion. As it was, he ended up in many battles with the Campbells, who were at this point on the side of the government. He ended up fighting at different times in England, Ireland and Scotland. Although supposedly under the command of the duke of Montrose, who had himself started out on the opposing Covenanting side, Coll Citach, or Colkitto as he was sometimes known, was effectively his own commander much of the time.

Coll always had a piper with him on campaign. The skirl of the pipes was a great way of inspiring the clan warriors, and the pipers were of course themselves seasoned warriors. One time, when Coll and his men were planning an attack on the castle of Duntroon on Loch Crinan, which was held by the Campbells, the piper had gone close to the castle to check out the lie of the land. He was captured by the Campbells, who were manning the fort, and taken to the castle itself to be interrogated. Now, the piper was well aware that the plan was to attack Duntroon from the sea at night and that it had been planned to happen that very night.

On reaching the castle, he immediately realised that the place was overflowing with fighting men. The castle had been sent considerable reinforcements and, if Coll and his men attacked this number, they would be slaughtered. They were heading straight into certain death. The piper was asked if he would tell of his leader's plans and, when he refused, the Campbell who was in charge of the garrison accepted that he would not betray his clansmen. Now this Campbell, like most of his clan, was little different from the men in other clans and was particularly fond of piping. He didn't have a piper in the castle and had been without music for over a week. So he asked the MacDonald piper if he would play him a tune.

'Och, aye, I'll play a tune for you,' replied the piper.

His bagpipes, confiscated on his capture, were brought to him. He accompanied the Campbell up to the battlements of the castle, the better to hear the pipes. 'Right, strike up a tune,' said the commander, while half a dozen of his men kept an eye on the piper, just in case he decided to do something rash. Highland warriors were known for their courage and many a man had gone to certain death in the knowledge that he had hurt his enemies. The notion of sacrifice was one which came easy to such men. But the piper had no intention of trying to attack the Campbells with his bare hands; he had a much better weapon – the pipes themselves.

Just as he reached the battlements, Coll and his men in their birlinns were rowing up Loch Crinan with muffled oars. They had laid their plans carefully and were sure they could triumph over the limited garrison at the castle. For once, their intelligence had let them down.

Up on the battlements the piper started to play. Out on the loch the MacDonalds heard the sound. Coll held up his hand and all the rowers stopped. Drifting out over the still waters of the loch in the dark night came the sound of a sad pibroch, 'Colla mo run' (Coll my love). Coll thought this was strange – why would a Campbell be playing that? Suddenly, in the middle of the pibroch, the pipe tune changed. The tune was interrupted by a brisk series of nervous-sounding notes – like an alarm. Then the pibroch started again. Still the rowers waited. After less than a minute the short, staccato tune broke in again. All at once, Coll understood. It was a warning! Their piper had somehow got hold of his pipes and was letting them know they shouldn't go ahead with the attack. Something was wrong. Standing in the lead birlinn, Coll gave a signal and, as quietly as they had come, the birlinns slipped away into the night to where they had come from.

Back on the battlement, the commander was puzzled. What

was this piper doing, breaking into a fine tune like that with a sort of . . . a warning. Just at that, a man came running onto the battlements.

'Captain,' he panted, 'there are birlinns in the loch. It is Coll Citach and his men, but they have turned back and are leaving.'

The captain understood; in a blind rage he drew his sword and thrust it straight through the bag of the pipes and into the piper's heart.

Out on the loch, Coll and his men heard the music come to an end with a terrible squeak, and knew the fate of their kinsman. Loyal to the last, he had saved his chief and his relations from what they now realised would have been a disastrous situation.

Cutach and the Caterans

In ancient clan life, all the able bodied men of the community were effectively warriors. Boys were trained in martial arts from a very early age, first being taught how to fight with short staves and gradually progressing till they learned the Highland arts of swordplay. Pipers, like smiths and other important members of clan society, were all fighting men. They were in fact warriors. The chance to show off their skill, bravery and honour came in one of the most dramatic aspects of clan life – the raiding of other clans' cattle. Cattle were the standard measure of movable wealth within Highland society and the 'lifting' of cattle gave the warriors a chance to show off their skills. A successful cattle raid need not always involve battle, but the participants were all ready, if not eager, for battle if it came. The raiders were long known as caterans, an old Gaelic word which translates best as warrior, but which, in the final years of Highland clan society, was used by the Lowlanders to mean nothing more than thief. There was some truth to this, for, as the ancient Highland warrior way of life died out, the traditional inter-clan raiding was increasingly replaced by raiding the Lowlands.

By the eighteenth century the Lowlands were essentially peaceful; few people carried or even had weapons. Raiding the rich farming areas adjoining the Highland glens meant relatively easy pickings for men who had been trained since childhood in this type of activity. This ongoing raiding, of course, merely served to increase the desire of the government to bring the Highlands under control – something they had been trying to do for more than half a millennium in one way or another. To the Highlander 'lifting' cattle was the proper use of his martial skills and an integral part of his life, whereas to the Lowlanders it was simply theft. The cattle-raiding had been going on for many hundreds of years and generally happened in September, after the harvest was in and there was time for the clan warriors to show off their skills and bravery. Every young man who might grow up to be a clan chief had to prove himself by leading just such a raid. Just as in later times the whisky smugglers would come down into the Lowlands with their convoys of Highland garrons (ponies) carrying barrels of whisky, often led by a piper, so the caterans would have a piper with them to play them back onto their ancestral lands after a successful raid.

In order to prevent constant hostility, and the risk of an ongoing blood feud, the Highlanders rarely, if ever, raided nearby clans and would travel long distances, sometimes well over a hundred miles, to lift cattle. However, although it was a fine and honourable thing to follow the cateran way, those being raided were generally just as skilled and brave, and generally had a raiding history of their own. It wasn't only the raiders who used pipers, as a tale from Strathardle in Perthshire makes clear.

Back in the fifteenth century, John Reid of Cutach was a man of some wealth and standing in the area and, despite being on the small side, was known for having a bit of a swagger. He even had his own piper, Sandy Robertson. He liked to do things in style and, even when off in the hills checking on his flocks, would sometimes take his piper with him to keep him company and to play him a tune or two when he felt like it. One day he was out in the hills with the piper when they saw in the distance a group of eighteen caterans driving a herd of lifted cattle north. Cutach recognised them as coming from over in Lochaber and realised the cattle they were driving might belong to one of his neighbours, or even himself.

He was a canny man, Cutach, and quickly figured out that by the time he or his piper could go and gather enough men from Strathardle to try and take the cattle back, the caterans would be well on their way into the mountain passes. In fact, they might not catch them up before nightfall and, once they were onto another clan's lands, there could be complications. So he decided he would have to act himself, and pretty quickly too.

'Right, Sandy,' he said to the piper, 'we cannot let these Lochaber men get away with the cattle. We will have to stop them.'

'But there're only the two of us,' replied the piper, 'and there're eighteen of them. You are surely not suggesting we offer them fair swordplay, are you?' He was asking if Cutach meant to challenge their best swordsman to fight one on one, the winner taking the cattle – a situation that was not that unusual.

'No, I don't think they would be for accepting that,' replied Cutach. 'But we have a weapon they don't,' he continued, with a smile. 'What is that?' asked Sandy.

'You,' said Cutach, grinning broadly. 'Now, here's what we will do . . .'

Only a few minutes later the caterans heard a noise behind them. They turned to see a kilted figure waving a sword on the top of a knoll. Suddenly, from behind him, came the sound of the bagpipes. The man turned and called out, 'We have them, lads; come on; there're less than twenty of them. We have them. Ewan, take your men up the burn on the left and head them off. Come on the rest of you, follow me.'

As the man ran down the hill towards them the pipes blew louder and the caterans looked at each other. The men behind them had already split into two groups. If they tried to let some run ahead with the cattle it would leave too few of them to put up much of a resistance to two different lots of fighting men. And the man had said that they were less than twenty – he clearly though they would be easy pickings. There must be at least forty or more of them.

As the piper struck up a battle march, Cutach ran up to the top of the hill and shouted, 'There they are, lads! Onwards! Some of you run ahead up the burn and get in front of them; we'll take them from behind.'

Now, Highland warriors were always known for their bravery, sometimes to the point of foolhardiness, but discretion is always the better part of valour and the raiders realised they could always come back another time. So, with only a few words, they left the cattle and ran off at full speed into the hills, sure that they were being pursued by a large force.

Behind them, Cutach told Sandy to keep playing and walk after the fleeing caterans for half a mile or so, then come back to him.

Then they gathered up the cattle and, with some difficulty, there being only the two of them, herded them back down to Strathardle, where they found men gathering to chase after the caterans. But there was no need: Cutach had seen them off with only himself and his trusty piper. Many a night the story was told and many a glass of uisge beatha was downed in a toast to John Reid of Cutach.

Odds and Ends

⇒◆⇐

There are so many tales abut pipers in Scottish tradition that some of them are difficult to fit into any particular category. Here we have a story of lifelong friendship; one about a practical joke on a piper; a sad story of commitment above and beyond the call of duty; and we finish off with a section about Queen Victoria and the pipes. The romanticisation of Scottish culture that took place in Victorian times has led to a modern realisation of the kitsch aspect of our culture that is described as 'tartan and shortbread', but, whether or not Victoria is responsible for this, there can be little doubt of her personal commitment to all things Scottish, including John Brown.

The Two Pipers

Early in the nineteenth century two lads lived at the west end of Strathglass, to the southwest of Inverness. They were called Hugh Simpson and Duncan Moir. They were great pals and did everything together, whether it was going to the school, looking after the cattle or cutting peats for the fire. One was never seen without the other from morning till night and they were in and out of each other's houses all the time. Summer or winter, spring or autumn, the two young lads were inseparable. At a young age they had both been set to learn how to play the pipes and, even when they were quite young, both mastered the pibroch known as 'The Old Woman's Lullaby', which remained a favourite of theirs all

209

their lives; they would often play it one after the other, and sometimes together.

Now, as was common in those days, they were both members of large families and on leaving school had no choice but to work for a living. Having lots of brothers and sisters meant that their families had no hope of being able to afford to support them while they learned a trade. They talked long and hard about what they should do. In truth, there weren't that many options open to them. Apart from joining the army, they could find work as labourers on a farm, or go to a city for work or, like so many other young Scots before them, they could go to sea, either as a fisherman or on a merchant ship. But there was one option they had that wasn't open to all.

Just as they were finishing their schooling, a recruitment party from the Cameron Highlanders was in Strathglass. As always, the government needed more soldiers for their Highland regiments. But they also needed a steady supply of pipers. When the recruiting sergeant heard that these two fit young lads were well on the way to becoming competent pipers he went out of his way to convince them of the benefits of a life wearing the king's colours. So, after much discussion the two lads, somewhat reluctantly, decided to enlist as pipers. There were tearful farewells with their families, both their mothers frightened they were never going to see their sons again, while their fathers stood by putting a brave face on things. Then off they set for the garrison at Fort George overlooking the Moray Firth, to learn the business of being pipers in the British army.

After their basic training, which took quite a few months, in which they mastered the intricacies of drilling as well as extending their piping skills, they were sent abroad with their regiment and for a long time no word of them came back to Strathglass. The two lads saw service under the hot sun of India and other parts of the far-flung British empire. They were often in the thick of the action and always kept a weather eye out for one another. So it came about that they survived twenty years of soldiering, after which they were discharged and returned to Invernessshire. They were entitled to their army pensions, which they could draw quarterly at Beauly, and headed back to Strathglass to settle down to a quieter life.

At first they stayed with relatives, of whom they had plenty in the area, while they got themselves sorted out. They were fortunate to get a croft each, what with the Lowland sheepmen beginning to take over so much of the land, but retired soldiers always had a bit of an advantage when it came to dealing with the big landowners, or any kind of official. The lands that they got were hardly first-class so, in addition to their farming, they were both on the look-out for any work that might come their way. Their pensions were small and farming was hard. But compared to many they weren't too badly off, and after a while both of them managed to find themselves a wife.

Still, their friendship held strong and they would often go to each other's houses for an evening of telling old tales and playing the pipes, usually till they were told to pack it in by their wives. There was a smooth green level patch above Duncan's house and he would often play his pipes there of an evening after working his croft. And, as often as not, the old favourite, 'The Old Woman's Lullaby', would be his choice. Hugh too had never lost his love for the piece and they often joked about playing it at each other's funeral. Both would in time be buried in the old burial ground of Clachain Comar in the glen below Duncan's croft.

This led other people to say, 'Don't be daft; only one of you will be able to do that.' However, it was like a private joke between the two of them. They both had families, who in their turn grew into adults. As was the case in so many parts of the Highlands, some of them were forced away to work and live in the cities. Still, the two old pipers lived with their wives in their crofts in Strathglass and for many years they made the effort to

211

visit each other and play their pipes, swap stories of their adventures abroad, and take pleasure in each other's company, as they had all their lives.

It was just about thirty years after they had returned from the army that Duncan died peacefully in his sleep. He had had a good life and was mourned by many, but by none more than his lifelong friend Hugh. At his funeral in Clachain Comair, Hugh played 'The Old Woman's Lullaby' with the tears streaming down his cheeks. Still, despite his loss and his advancing years, he played the tune as well as ever he had.

Afterwards, back at Duncan's house with the rest of the funeral party, the conversation turned to the idea the two of them had had about playing at each other's funerals.

After a drink or two, an old friend said, 'Ach, Duncan will not be playing at your funeral now, will he?'

Hugh replied, 'I will not be long for this life myself and can tell you this: Duncan will be waiting at the gates of paradise to welcome me – and he would think nothing of nipping back to play at his old friend's funeral. He was as true a friend as a man could have.'

Most there just put this down to the emotions of the day and an old man's fond memories of his pal. However, it was only a short while after that Hugh too went to meet his maker. People saw that an era was passing in Strathglass with the death of its pipers. Times were changing; more and more people were heading for the cities and the glens were slowly emptying of their greatest treasure, the Highland people themselves.

Hugh too was to be buried at Clachain Comair, to lie near his old friend for eternity. They were both survived by their wives, who intended to join them there in their turn. Though many of their bairns would never return to sleep beside their ancestors in Strathglass. A piper was, of course, needed for Hugh's funeral and word was sent to an old friend, whom they themselves had both taught many years before in the Cameronians.

When he arrived he was told that the tune he was to play would be the old favourite of both the Strathglass pipers, 'The Old Woman's Lullaby'. This he was delighted to do. It was a moist morning with wisps of mist blowing through the glen and the mountain-tops wreathed in cloud. When Hugh's coffin was lowered into the ground before the assembled men at the funeral, the piper began to play the famous pibroch.

Right enough he was playing 'The Old Woman's Lullaby', but the sons of the old pipers and many of the other locals were taken aback by his rendition. After Hugh and Duncan had left the army it appeared he had fallen into some pretty bad piping habits. There were some mutterings at the way he was playing the pibroch — some said it might have done for the army but wasn't a patch on how Hugh and Old Duncan had always played it. Others whispered this would be a great disappointment to both the old pipers looking down from heaven and that, all in all, it was a pretty bad do all round. The piper himself, concentrating on the tune, didn't notice the stirring in the crowd. Then something happened.

From the level green field where Duncan had so often walked while playing the pibroch came the sound of pipes. The tune was 'The Old Woman's Lullaby', and the crowd all turned to look. This caught the piper's eye and he stopped playing. The sound of the pibroch, played exactly as Duncan and Hugh had performed it, was drifting down from the ground above. And there, just over a half a mile away on the green level spot above Duncan's house that had become known as Duncan's Green over the years, could clearly be seen a kilted figure with the pipes over his shoulder, marching back and forth just as Duncan had done for so many years. People stood in shock and wonder, many with tears rolling down their cheeks. As the tune came to an end they turned to each other saying, 'Did you see that?' and 'Could it really be . . .?' and, 'Was it Duncan himself?' and 'That must have been Duncan; he always promised he would play at Hugh's funeral, you know.'

They all looked back up to the spot where the figure had been pacing, but there was nothing to be seen and nothing to be heard. The glen had gone deathly still. As the funeral party headed back to Hugh's house the consensus was clear: 'It must have been Duncan – it sounded just like him,' said one. Another chipped in, 'Well they always said they would play at each other's funeral, right enough.'

Back at the house, the piper himself, who had been more than a little shaken by what had happened, calmed himself with a stiff whisky and added his own take on the situation. 'Ay, it surely sounded like Duncan. It was just as he played the tune. I should have played it that way myself. I am ashamed to say I have let the tune go a bit over the years.'

'Well,' interjected a local man who had known both pipers well, 'I don't know about you, but I reckon if you had played it as you should have you wouldn't have had to bother Old Duncan into coming back.'

All there were regular Highland church-goers, but in the Scottish mountains the old ways and the old beliefs die hard. No one was in any doubt what had happened, despite the presence of the minister. Anyway, the story spread like wildfire and Duncan's Green was visited by a great many people while his wife lived, and even after. No piping was ever heard from there again, though at the funerals of the pipers' respective wives there were a few who cast the odd look up the hill to the site of Duncan's Green.

About forty years after Hugh was buried, a local man, William Alexander, came back to visit the west end of Strathglass. He had been living in Australia, where he had gone just a short while after Hugh's funeral. He himself was a very fine piper indeed and had had more than the odd lesson from the two old pipers in his youth. He visited various old people still remaining in the glen and a few cousins and other relatives in the surrounding area. As these things have always happened, the talk would turn to story and, on a couple of occasions, the return of the piper to Duncan's Green came up. The story of the ghost piper was well known and popular and had been told over and over again. Mind you, there were many who hadn't heard 'The Old Woman's Lullaby' itself in many years. It was at a gathering in his cousin Davie's house that William said, 'Well, I could give the tune a go; I have never forgotten it.' He then proceeded to play the old pibroch exactly as he had been taught it all those years before.

As soon as he had finished, Davie burst in excitedly, 'That's it, just the way Old Duncan and Hugh played it. It's like the ghost piper was here amongst us.'

And at that the story came out. William had been asked to play at the funeral by a cousin of Hugh's and was on his way with his pipes, in full Highland dress, to Hugh's house to accompany the coffin to the burial ground, when he saw the army piper was there before him. He was more than a little disappointed and, when the rest of the party set off for the Clachain Comair, he went off on his own up to Duncan's Green. He watched from a distance and, when he heard that the piper was making a mess of the tune, being young and maybe a bit headstrong, he knew just what he should do. He marched up and down the green playing the exact rendition he had been taught, note for note. He then ducked into the bracken so no one would see it was him. He then caught up with the men coming from the burial ground and, as he had been asked by one of the cousins to play, no one thought anything of the fact he had his pipes with him. In fact they all thought he had been among the crowd in the graveyard. When the word got out about William's story there were those who said he was making it up. They preferred to keep telling the story of the piper who came back from the dead to play at his best friend's funeral. You can't beat a good story.

A Practical Joke on a Piper

One time in the 1850s an Edinburgh lawyer was spending a week in a hotel on the west coast. He appeared to be a man of somewhat pompous demeanour and he spoke very slowly and precisely, but it was just a front; underneath it he had a wicked sense of humour. He had been coming to this particular hotel for a few years and had got to know one of the regulars at the hostelry, a Highland piper by the name of McGlashan, who stayed there when he was in the area. McGlashan had what we would now call a regular gig, playing for the tourists, most of whom were English. But there was a smattering of Europeans drawn to Scotland by the growing tourist industry, stimulated to a large extent by the romance of Sir Walter Scott's novels. Now, the piper was a trusting soul and a pretty fair piper but the lawyer, always on the lookout for a victim for a practical joke, decided the piper was just the man. He wasn't malicious, but he liked a good laugh and a good story; and if one could lead to the other then that pleased him even more.

One evening it was raining and he was looking through an old cupboard in the dining room of the inn, for lack of anything much better to do, when he noticed a set of old and broken pipes lying on a shelf. He didn't think much of it at the time but later that evening, while supping a glass of port, he had a thought which made him smile. He would play a trick on the piper. For his plan to work he had to wait till the evening meal of the house was to be haggis – the 'warm, reekin, rich' national dish of Auld Scotland. In the meantime, he took the young lad who did odd jobs about the place into his confidence. Giving him a few shillings, he told him to wait till he was given the signal, at which point his job would be to lift McGlashan's pipes when he wasn't looking. He also paid the young lad to find a set of ribbons to match those on the piper's set; they would be needed later. The day came round when it was announced that that night's dinner would be Scotland's national dish; the Edinburgh lawyer was asked if he would read Burns's 'Address to the Haggis'. Being of a mischievous frame of mind, the lawyer had tipped off both the landlord and the dominie, the local schoolmaster, who also took his meals in the hotel. They were having real trouble keeping straight faces as they all sat at the table.

The landlady came into the room carrying a large platter, the contents of which were giving off a rich, meaty, spicy smell. There were a few appreciative noises; then the piper looked at the platter. There was a set of pipes, the bag split open to reveal the spicy haggis spilling onto the plate.

The piper took one look and sprang to his feet. 'God have mercy on us, you are not serving us up boiled bagpipes, woman!' He looked a little closer and, seeing what he took to be his ribbons, let forth a stream of vicious imprecations and curses in Gaelic.

Switching to English, with a wild look in his eyes, he yelled, 'Who has done this terrible thing? What nasty person has insulted me by destroying my pipes?' He almost burst into tears at the thought of having lost his bagpipes. 'Who was it?' he demanded, 'Who has done this terrible thing?'

'Och, dinnae fash,' said a travelling cattle dealer at the table, who was also in on the joke. 'Let's just eat. I wouldn't give up a mouthful of this sumptuous dish for aw the music that ever came from the instrument, Mr McGlashan.'

The dominie chimed in: 'This will be what they call a real musical feast!'

'Well,' said the lawyer, 'it'll probably give us aw wind. Och, sit down, McGlashan man, you yourself have said it often enough – a fu bag makes a good loud drone.'

By this time there were chuckles and suppressed snorts all round the table, and the piper, standing at the side of the table, still bursting with anger, was beginning to realise that something was going on. Everything was not as it appeared to be. He was looking questioningly between the pipes and the company assembled around the big table. He couldn't fathom why they were all so pleased that his pipes had been destroyed.

Just then, the door opened and the young lad came in on cue with the original pipes. The entire company burst into laughter, apart from McGlashan himself, who was so relieved at getting his pipes back in one piece that a tear sprang from his eye. Grabbing the pipes, he looked them over, patting and almost caressing them as he did so. He filled his bag and played a spring, but he was so upset that he could barely keep a tune going and was told to sit down. After the meal, when the punch bowl came out, he began to relax and after a glass or two he began to appreciate the humour of the trick played on him. Then he took up his pipes and this time managed to toss off a few tunes to general pleasure. However from that day forward Piper McGlashan could never again could look at a plate of haggis without suffering palpitations.

The Piper and the Minister

Donald was a piper and an only son. His mother Annie had a tendency to fuss over him. As she saw him off to a dance or a wedding she would always say, 'Now, Donald, don't forget your poor old mother.' The first time she said this he asked what she meant and she told him, 'Well for every glass of whisky you drink you should put one in the mull (bag) for me.' She wasn't wanting to drink the stuff from the bag when he got home – well, would you? – but she knew this would slow his drinking down considerably and, after all, it had long been believed that a drop or two in the mull was good for the pipes.

Now, as has often been the case, jobs were in short supply in the Highlands at this time and Donald decided to follow a well-trodden path: he went to become an army piper at Fort George, overlooking the Moray Firth. He was sent abroad to India, where he was involved in several battles, the last of which saw him being shot in the head. Though he recovered to some extent, he was never the same again and the army soon let him go. He returned to live with his parents with a small pension and they tried their best to look after him.

He was easily depressed and his family and neighbours were always keeping an eye out for the poor piper. One day, however, he got away from the house without being seen and went off to the nearby river to drown himself. The first his family knew of it was when he came back, saying the water was too cold to drown himself! This terrified his parents and they summoned a doctor; it wasn't too long before Donald was sent off to the asylum at Montrose, a long way off from his home near Inverness.

About a year later he was allowed home, his condition much improved, and he was full of enthusiasm about getting back to playing the pipes. Soon he was playing at the odd social occasion, but everyone was very careful to ensure that he didn't drink. It was thought this would be too dangerous for him. Though he was back playing the pipes, he wasn't completely well: he still got headaches and tended at times to be a bit distracted; his concentration, on anything other than the pipes, was variable. As he had nothing much else to fill his life, he played all the time and, if anything, his playing improved. The problem his family had was in getting him to stop, but they were all pleased that Donald was doing so well.

He developed the habit of strolling through the village in the evening, playing his pipes. This was something that many of the villagers looked forward to and a lot of the younger lads in particular were very appreciative. Sadly, though, not everyone thought that Donald's playing was a boon to the place. When the crunch came it came from a surprising corner. One particular late summer evening, after a long hot beautiful day, Donald strode down through the village, kilt swinging, playing a beautiful set of marches. Many people were at their doors and there was applause and a bit of cheering from the villagers for their local piper. However, Donald, not surprisingly given his condition, hadn't noticed that it was a Sunday! Now, this was in the nineteenth century, hundreds of years since the fanatics of the Presbyterian church had outlawed music and dancing in Scotland. The local minister was of that same, sad, puritanical way of thinking. The piper was profaning the Sabbath! He could not stand by and allow this obscenity! Never mind that this was a man damaged in the service of his country, and a man who intended harm to no one. He had profaned the Sabbath and had to be made to pay for it.

The minister laid a complaint to the local magistrate, who called in the police. The minister was adamant that something had to be done, so the police came to the village and took poor Donald away. His family were distraught. And they had every right to be. For Donald the piper was sent back to the asylum and never returned to play his pipes at home again.

Queen Victoria and the Pipes

Scotland's modern tourist industry is often said to have been started by Sir Walter Scott when he organised the royal visit of George IV in 1822. In the early nineteenth century, the highly romanticised vision of Scotland that Scott helped to create appealed to the middle and upper classes of both Scotland and England. This new vision of the romantic Highlander, with his colourful language and dress, his supposedly feudal loyalty to his chief and his closeness to nature, replaced the terrifying figure of the warlike Gael that had been so prevalent in the mid-eighteenth century. Then they had been seen as barbarians, ever ready to descend on

Lowland Scotland and England. Now, after brutal campaigns of cultural genocide and ethnic cleansing through the Highland clearances, in an echo of the eighteenth-century idea of the 'noble savage', the fearsome Highland warriors had become a fantasy for tourists.

When Queen Victoria came to the throne she became infatuated with Scotland's rugged grandeur and supposed romantic past. The upshot of this was that she bought Balmoral; the day of the great Highland hunting estates had arrived. Some people like to think that these great estates are in some way a direct development from the Highland past. Nothing could be further from the truth: where the hills used to sustain people, great sheep runs were installed. The creation of the Highland hunting estates was just as new a development.

However, Queen Victoria herself was well and truly bitten with the Scottish bug and very keen on all things Scottish. When on a visit to the marquis of Breadalbane at his home in Taymouth Castle in Perthshire in 1842, she was very taken with the playing of piper John Ban Mackenzie. It wasn't just his playing that attracted her, but the figure he made in full Highland dress, playing gold-mounted pipes. The irony of the British queen adoring the very dress her grandfather had outlawed in the Disarming Act of 1746 was quite lost on her. The attitude of the times can be seen in what she said after her welcome at Taymouth Castle with fireworks, volleys of gunshots and the skirl of the pipes: 'It seemed as if a great chieftain in older feudal times was receiving his sovereign. It was princely and romantic.' It was also utter fantasy, as the Highlands of Scotland were never feudal – in fact there might be some argument for suggesting that Victoria herself and the owners of the great hunting estates effectively installed a late form of feudalism. And, if great chieftains came up against their 'sovereign' in the Highlands, it was usually in battle.

After returning to London, she wrote to Breadalbane asking if he could recommend a piper as good as John Ban to become the royal piper. The way stories are told in piping circles, it is hardly surprising to hear that Breadalbane knew John Ban was the best piper of his generation, so asked him if he would like to go and work for the queen. His reported reply reeks of the romanticism that was so prevalent at the time: 'I do not wish for a better master than yourself.' The portrayal of Mackenzie as some kind of feudal vassal is part of that fantasy world of Highland gentlemen and willing servants so beloved of the Victorians. However, Mackenzie did not make the move to work for the queen.

In fact, the queen's first piper was none other than Angus Mackay, one of the most intriguing figures in nineteenth-century piping, appointed in 1843. In his critique of the MacCrimmon legend, Alexander Campsie makes much of Mackay's later struggles with madness, possibly brought on by syphilis, and suggests that he was something of a conman. There is no doubt that Mackay was instrumental in developing the legend of the MacCrimmons, but he was also the winner of the piping contest in Edinburgh in 1835 in his early twenties, no mean feat. He must surely have been a fine piper. However, as Campsie notes, there are anomalies in the book of music produced under Mackay's name, *A Collection of Piobaireachd, or Highland Pipe Music*. It is from this time on the MacCrimmon legend really took off, and Campsie has a case in his criticism of the book. As I have already said, stories have a life and a relevance of their own and the various tales of the MacCrimmons presented here have their place.

Jamie Burnie

Another piper who was in Queen Victoria's employment was James McHardy of Burnside, near Corgarff, better known as

Jamie Burnie. In 1877 the queen was looking for an apprentice piper at Balmoral; the fourteen-year-old Jamie was chosen for the position from several young pipers living in the area. By this stage, the queen's piper was a man called Ross and he had a particular method of teaching. If the young lad made a mistake while practising on the chanter, he was punished by a whack from the maestro's chanter. He long remembered the pain of having a finger whanged between two chanters and, ever after, maintained that it certainly stopped him making the same mistake twice!

One of the perks of the job as apprentice to the queen's piper was the opportunity of travelling abroad. Jamie went with the queen to France and Italy. He found that the Italians in particular were somewhat wary of the bagpipe. One day he went for a walk, taking his pipes with him. He decided to play a few tunes in the piazza of the nearby town and soon attracted a small crowd, both children and adults. As he played, the people came closer and closer, intrigued by this powerful sound. As soon as Jamie finished, in a jocular fashion he pointed the big drone at the Italians, all of whom disappeared like lightning!

It was also in Italy that he had an experience that shows Queen Victoria in a slightly unusual light. Part of Jamie's duties was to act as a sort of valet to the queen, carrying her umbrella or cloak, and such things as hampers and blankets at picnics. She liked the young lad and one day she took him out shopping with her. For once, John Brown, with whom Jamie did not get on, was absent. In those days it was still possible for royalty to travel around almost like ordinary people. This day the queen went to a little antique shop with Jamie in tow. The proprietor of the shop, who had a fair command of English, was not fooled by the alias the queen was travelling under, knowing quite well who this black-clad woman was. He was understandably a bit nervous and, when the queen asked to see a certain item on a high shelf, he went and fetched a small set of stepladders. Climbing the ladder while trying to keep up a conversation over his shoulder with his illustrious guest was too much for the man. He got to the top of the steps and reached for the object, still trying to talk to the queen. All at once he came crashing down, pulling the entire contents of the shelf on top of himself. At once the queen fled the shop, closely followed by young Jamie. There in the street the queen burst into a fit of laughter, lasting several minutes. Contrary to what has often been said of Victoria, she obviously had a sense of humour.

Despite the queen's fondness for the young lad, his strained relations with John Brown, who it appears might have been jealous of the young piper, led to him to decide that he would have to quit her service. Accordingly, on handing in his notice, he asked for a testimonial from Brown. It was a remarkable testimonial which read: 'James McHardy left. Gave no offence. Signed, John Brown.' Smarting at the slight, Jamie tore it up the moment he left Balmoral.

In later years, despite different employment, he never ceased playing his pipes, winning many competitions, and going on to become a judge at many Highland Games, particularly the Lonach Games. For a while he was a conductor of the new trams in Aberdeen, his piping skills coming in handy on the day the very first of the trams ran. There, on the front of the upper deck of this new-fangled invention going through the streets of Aberdeen was Jamie Burnie playing his pipes! While a young man he also learned to play the fiddle and went on to record several broadcasts on both instruments for BBC Radio in Aberdeen in the 1920s and '30s. His epitaph in the *Bon-Accord* newspaper in 1938 referred to him as a 'prince of pipers'.

A Big Blaw

In Scots 'to blaw' can have the meaning of to boast as well as to blow. In the late seventeenth century there was a boatman called

Alisdair Mor Grant, who was reputed to be the best boatman ever. His vessel was a curragh, or skin boat, and in his hands it could perform remarkable feats. He once went to London along with the laird of Grant, and carried his curragh all the way. There, his boating skills were greatly appreciated and his bonnet was filled with silver. But young Alisdair was wanting home and it is said he astounded the Londoners by handing over all the money he had been given to his chief, asking him to give it to his wife to buy pins!

He was so well-regarded by the Grant that he had his picture painted and it was hung alongside a portrait of Grant's piper. Tradition has not preserved the piper's name, but there is a story told of him that he took on a bet that had the better of him. He was well-known as a piper and, like many of his kind, was a strong healthy man, well used to the mountain life and extremely fit. His ego, however, got the better of him one day when he took a bet that he could march from Inverness to Castle Freuchie and three times round the castle without stopping. This would be some feat, as Castle Freuchie was a bit over twenty-five miles from the Highland capital. Anyway, the day came and the bold piper set out from Inverness, playing steadily as he went. By the time he had marched the six hours and more to Castle Freuchie his spirit was beginning to weaken. The tone of his piping had become coarse and he was missing the fingering of all too many notes. Still, he was marching; it was clear to all those who had come to the castle to watch him win his bet that he intended going on to the finish. As he went round the castle the first time his legs were seen to buckle, but he pulled himself up and carried on. His heart was pounding in his ears like a great drum and his eyesight was becoming blurred. As he began the second circuit of the castle the hushed onlookers realised something was going wrong. His eyes were entirely bloodshot, but still he kept marching and playing the pipes. A third time he completed the circuit, legs buckling and shoulders shaking, but complete it he did. The shouts and cries of triumph from his friends turned to groans of distress as the piper fell. His next pibroch was played to his ancestors.